small
lucidities

•

miriam
e.walsh

book 4 random series

ardornata
publishing

Cover art by Miriam E. Walsh
Book design by Miriam E. Walsh

ISBN 978-0-9836598-3-9

ardornata publishing
www.ardornatadesign.com

Table of Contents

About The Author

Miriam E. Walsh has worn many hats to pay the bills:
mental health worker at a detox unit, drafter in the engineering field
and graphic designer --- but she has always donned the hat of a
poet.

For many years, at her home on the south shore in Massachusetts,
she has tended to many writing projects, the culmination of which
is the Random Series of books. These poems have been written in
many places; lunch breaks, poetry readings, train rides and, yes,
car rides!

She has been published in U.M.Ph.! Prose Online and is a regular
fixture at local poetry venues including "Poetry: The Art Of Words
Mike Amado Memorial Series" in Plymouth, Massachusetts.

Miriam E. Walsh has an BS Degree in Psychology from
Bridgewater State College, where she also minored in art. She is
an accomplished photographer/visual artist and a member of the
Plymouth Arts Guild.

random series
book 1 : beautifully alien refraction
book 2 : primitive awe
book 3 : forced continuity
book 4 : small lucidities

quarantine 06

they'll look at my
eyes
from behind the glass,

a safe, zoo-like distance,

at the
the sunken ,
the stare,
a widening
that only lets in
more darkness,

a wild too wise,
too wizened,
to be allowed
in open air.

and they'll shake
their heads
in pity.
oh what
a pity

i hear it runs
in the family
poor dear, just gave up
she was just weak
all along

and numerous
other latex layers
and sanitizing clichés
of sanctifying damnations

thick enough
to dull the pierce

of my gaze;

and my muteness
will let them,

and let them
leave.

so we can be
at peace
in each others
quarantine.

the empty 07

i am here
i know i am
here

here   like sky
like star
like moon
here   like tree
like fish
like lowly worm
that leaf
that grass
that dragonfly

and as all these
like things
must die.

then i know
and suddenly

i am

not like
any of these

i know.

its a singularity
that tears
with every step
with every breath

until it is the beneath
within my eye

the darkness
that snares light,

the retinal self
the holographic me

this inner
that brings the outward
within

a skin
that loves
with the shape
of its empty.

another 07

haunted
by the
previous tenant,

her eyes
in casual study
of a ring,
its deep facets.

and a breath
escapes
releasing the risen,

a mnemonic shadow
crossing the sun
casting a shiver
in point for point
proportion

to every inch
of her skin.

it matched
her reflex
and
her ritual
of being,

a dark
for every lit

but it was
not her.
it was
another.

a before,
a once,

a never again.

that made her stare
out the window
in half

expectancy
too see

its feet on dewed grass,
its eyes full of days,

standing there.

but it was
her reflection.

without me 07

what keeps me lonely
makes me alone,

how the world sees
this form
this woman
this me.

even the flattering
is flattening.

a mother
with a taste
for everyone
else's
insatiability.

trained by a doll
and an easy-bake oven,

caretakers of humanity
and its dirty little secret:

that even the ones
with homes
have Stockholm's

especially those.

for there was always
the threat at the door

next door,
next channel,
next 10 second promo,

the taught
with the taut smile
that knew
and told you,
with tense pretenses,
that you would die
without

those pearly whites,
that shiny hair,
that perfect ass,
the detergent
that made anything clean.

that the rapist
would come
if you opened your mouth,

and all the ways
they make sure it
comes
true.

what keeps me lonely?
that earth is empty.
what makes me alone?
that i refuse to be

without me.

terra incognita 07

a silken sheet,
a light cool blanket
barely brushing
the end of my every hair,
shortening my breath
with its coddling
proximity.

the sun is a flashlight
to this self told story
and, a curious child,
I have refused
to go to sleep

but instead ,
a nascent
to this natal narrative,

I can feel the night
outside
and how
inadvertently illuminated
I am
before it.

I see its fingers
shaping my shelter,
this sky
inward
with a wanting.

in these words
I hear
inside my ears
drumming outward
with syllables
of familiar unknowns

and its flitting shadows
hiding and seeking
me
in the curved corners
of my eye,
racing across my retina
before I can
react
and convince myself
they are real

or that they are not.

catalyst 07

the cold
was less a care
than a catalyst.

it crystallized
her breath
into blue sparks
crackling upon
each syllable
by this ocean,
this nightly winter walk.

they followed this path
as any other night,

walking from
the dimness
toward a lamp
that hung
in careless suspension
over earth,
a yellow sun
in this spartan-edged
chill.

he didn't need
to see her face.
he had memorized
it
long ago.

with each step forward
he expected the same
as all sunrises

but into the light
each shades opposite
landscaped
her face into a
untried topography

its canyons,
its deserts,
its subterranean rivers

bellowing into lakes
with a sight,
worshipping this star
with a reflection
glistening
and
then listening
for an answer.

her skin burned
white hot,
a planet falling
into a fiery gravity,
razing the lines
from her face
until she was
only glow
with boiling oceans

and then it passed,
the light behind them.

and he had
a new face to learn.

desperate now 07

here it passes
an organism
a wit
with a label
that coincides
with a configuration
of lines
and
exhausted expressions.
of pink
on skeleton,
of genetics
that may
or may not
participate in a possibly
pointless parade
across time
with its progeny,

but for now
it works,
it walks,
it breathes,
but never speaks
about
what really is;

about this
only
desperate now.

hum 07

the wheels
under me.
the heater blowing.
the engine
feeding on our
forevers;

and leaving few left.

the distant
soar of a plane;
a light bulb
filament ringing.

a tvs whistle
and
ensuing babble.

my car keys
jingling like a chime
at every pothole.

a clock's tick.

a streetlamp
sputtering.

the silence coming.

famished 07

at night
i saw
a woman
feed a swan
as
it prayed and swooned
with sinuous stretch
upward,
a kissing
in the most greedy way
the bread from
her fingers
with the tips
and not the nails
careful,
gentle
as to a child,

and the dark ducks
barked and bellowed,
a slinking sea
waiting for the
castoff crumbs

of a god
being fed
by a god;

grace nurturing the
merely graceful.

the swan purred
for its supper
a cat
under a stroke
of suns fingers
it hissed
all these rivals back
from its territory,
from its privilege,
with omnipotent will
as the woman
still
fed it

all the same,

until it waddled away
fat and finished

yet still famished.

else 07

a broken mirror

these pieces
miniscule me
glaring
from the ground,
from hard edged puddles,

cutting the floor away
from my feet.

their shape
recording an impact
with
their spider,
their splintering
gleaming
red eyed and hard breathing
clones
of a raving thing

now still,

now staring
at someone else's
destruction

indeed
it was someone else
who did that

that saw that face,
that pulled from the wall
a now
that should never be.

but i will clean
it up

wrapping
the pieces carefully
in old newspapers
and other
newly created debris

and pushing them down

but still ripping
still existing

and impossible
to throw away.

hands 07

praying to
my fingers

the only useful
things
to hear
these words

so that they
can execute
what I need to do

and if not

execute me.

by my own hands
by my own hands

prying
me open

to get at all that
delicious empty
that savory
sense of being
salty upon my tongue

especially all those tears

predator
the world purrs
in the
sated satisfaction
of corpses

by our own. . .

red is
vivid and lives
in all of our blind-spots

the dead are
some else's

job
not mine

my coffee
my ipod
my church
my mosque
my synagogue
my demigod

the holy relics
the holy books

blunt objects
to beat the truth out

and ours in

without a single
drop of blood

on our own hands.

bathyal 07

this flood
this fluid
defense
saline and surreal
misinterpretation
of pain
for injury;

accumulating

building
a new base
a new bathyal

and the water
is rising.

that my eyes
can't tell

the difference.

cleansed with
these tides
of all debris
anticipated
there

but isn't

the dissipated
washing empty shores
the devastation
is the reflection;
the surface
of this sight.

and the part
that really sees,

the dark bottom
of these seas,

all these
sinking semblances
assembling

feline 07

part feline
part feeling

and with an
uninvested blink

stretched
across newspapers
that shriek
in
black and white
boldface serif

watch them leave.

but only creak
beneath my weight
and
blissful waiting

my limbs wading
through
a chorus of coruscation,
glittering dust storms
kicked up
by my careless carefree

and rise,
a migration
of small lucidities

escaping the syllables
they were trapped
within
and leave
silent and impotent
all those
violent vowels,
accosting consonants;

their ink fading
in this sun.

giddy 07

this giddy,
it is not good

nor even pleasant.

a gory thing
it gores
the wrinkles
into my skin
into my mind

and chews
on each nerve

and I twitch

with tears
with claws
with grating teeth
with that
fuckyoualldyingscreaming
allofyoudie
screaming...ihopeyou...

howcanyouhowcanyou (the
raped, the burning)
howcanyouhowcanyou (the
panic resurfacing)
howcanyouhowcanyou (the
waste....

howdareyou

(abulletspatteronawhitewall)

>how are you?
>I am fine.

reset
resettle
resolved
to my
resigned

just
eat well
eat less
fuck more
fuck them
god's flood is coming,
you should drink more
water.

the way
of the
just
justice

just ice

just I
c..........

this giddy.....

regular programming 07

my teeth are gnashing
my fingers crushing

upon nothing,
poor witless empty.

because
all of the deserving
are out of
my reach

but broadcasting
24hour news
of the
freshly fabricated.

this vacuum
carries their
vacuous vacant
to my ears

interrupting
this hush
with hypnotism
I am to
slackjaw swallow
because they flicker

with their
glowing
gloating
garble

of surrogate concern
in celebrity calamity

a dead platinum queen,
a poor rich girl
a bloated baby in a blue
suit
spitting fat tinged tirades
about how welfare
and all against warfare

will waste him
away

thoseingratefulliberalloonies
(but there's something I can
reach)
dontyoulovegodlovechil-
drenloveamerica
(just beyond my finger)
youcommunistplotflipflop
(a choice in well lit LED)
yougodless

(off)
()

too 07

a far
too efficient

if I had them anyway.
but speaking
requires

state of being
has counted
and discounted
every nerve
and found

two words
that I can manage
to put
together

too well

instead

an immunity
to impulse
a pulse
whose peaks are
too gradual,
for this graduate
of epochs of panic,
to detect.

a finger on my neck
to trace
the all

too regular
pattern of mere content-
ment

that I will never get
too quiet
too easy

too used
to.

to be mine.

a breath
too warm
to form words
too thin
for them
to travel

too far

evidence2 07

is hurt
quantitative

measured
in pulses and waves

seen with current instruments,
it is only
crudely observed

in the shortness
of my breath
the far away
here
of my eyes;

the silence
that answers
all of your questions.

and yet
quanta
can be counted,
bedbugs
seen on microbial mountains,
and a
never seen singularity
detected
as it dines.

but not this
apple ache
at my throat.

that fruit is a sin
I am supposed
to choke upon,

as all my worlds
are building behind it.

how many
laid end to end
will be
evidence?

no matter 07

this pink of sky,
this silhouette of now,
the dawn
that will wake us;

no matter the light
no matter the matter
no matter

just this
shadow,
and its edges
cutting the clouds.

the blue I breathe,
the moment continued,
this comfort
that allows sleep;

no matter the night
no matter the mother
no matter

just the cradle
coddling me
with in these clouds

flying
at hundreds of thousands
and still
still

and still slumbering

floating
upon a ocean of air
beneath black
that's looking back
as close as blanket
but staring through
with singular eyes
eating
each second

no matter
the sea upon my steps
a void rising
no matter
the sear of sun
I avoid seeing
no matter

a new clear
fissioning
fashioning
a new horizon

with our
unenlightened.

no matter

the difference 07

what's the difference
between
twelve
and
midnight

is it anything
more than dark

buildings built
of brittle bricks
or roads
of blacker tar?

are there different laws?
does dim erase ink?

is my skin
protected by light
so that the intensity
of the sun
shields me
from what
stars cannot

for all the burning

does some primal
fear of predator

now
give an excuse
to modern ones
that choose
to come

and this night
an option
to all else
to be blind
when fingers tear
at female flesh

why
do mouths not scream
but
only inquire
what she was doing

at such an hour;

what is the difference?

tongue thai'd 07

an element
ionized
and whizzing by
in the form
of a skateboarder,

arms up,
pierced stare,
straight
into the wind

as the light
refracts
in my pinot.

there are stars
at the bottom,
glittering lamps
captured there

and i will drink
down to them,

borrowing
a numb warmth
that comes from
not quite forgetting
but at least
not remembering
so frequently.

and these spices,
the burn,
the sweet,
the rapturous

in between,
they are arguing for
my attention
the way that instruments
debate
and create symphony.
they overwhelm
all the mundane
flavors
before them

and make me

drink more;

holding my glass
to my eye
like a galileo
about to be punished
for what i see

holding it to my lips,
as persephone
knowing it will
tie me
to where i am,

which is not so bad.

beneath a wine
sky
and a wine
haze,

i taste in all the ways
genuine.

train 07

my thoughts are
as these
train-cars floating
at still speeds.
one barely tethered
to the next.
tied only by inertia
and wreckage
if I stop them too soon.

without,
dollhouse landscapes
passing,
their whisper more muted
by my thundering roar;

within ,
each face
a study in solitude
staring into themselves,
what they have to do;
why;
this day,
this work,
this worry without warrant,

the minutes and hours
they trade for lives,

a shadow cast by
a unseen shrinking sun
a flickering fluorescent
of all things beneath
this wistful want.

its outline is a shadow
peeking out from
under well worn shoes.

a child screams.
"look!"
the same roads
the same houses

but each eye will look,

old reflections
upon new mirrors.

"weeeeeeeee!"

and I remember,
all the faces did.

the smirks
radiated outward;
centered upon
another sun,

listening as a mother
explained
that the houses
are not running,
they just seem to be;
how we are not flying
it just looks that way

each question
barely waiting
for her answer
to finish.

other lips mouth
with glinting glances
across aisles
the obvious
as if just discovered.

and the train
tilts and squirms
a burrowing worm
chewing up rust
and spitting out
new momentum

and widening eyes

hearing nows 07

this moment creased,
now unfolds
with each unidentified sound
that becomes footsteps,
a pattern of creaks
that
i stop
to lsten to .

me,
a hollow
haunting the ghosts
with nouns
unknown to even them.
hearing nows
expanding
with
my articulate art
of unsaying,
just before
that look
that gleam
of the living upon death

when its not
unwilling.

when marrow
no longer feeds the blood
but is driven dry
by all the days' suns

and too many noons
have had my shadow
standing
in my feet,
waiting
pre-pounced
and pondering
my splinters
upon its teeth.

[un]just 07

I used to
feel joy, now just
not sad.

I used to feel love, now just
not hate,

I used to believe, now I just
don't know.

the world just
does not forgive
my life or just
living
this long;

my birth or just
not dying.

a humanity stolen
in just
small enough increments
and endless ends

to go just
unnoticed.

I just
do not get to,
I just
do not get to,

I just . . .

bored again 07

I find myself

less and less,
more or less,
lessened

by all these lessons.

the gods that
whisper blasphemies
inside of me.

forced in by
my ears,
my mouth ,
my eyes,

or otherwise;

those lies,

all those
I love you's
that loved nothing.

these involuntary humilities,
these purposeful futilities.

all the ways
living will kill me,
all the while
dying
has given me
reason

to live,

now that the world
is busy ending,

now that
all the dinosaurs
are harvested
or in cabinet positions
advising upon
the next extinction.

waiting upon
rupture or rapture;
awed at god,
as ape at the moon,
dangling
midday, midsky
illuminating unknowns
I'd rather forget.

the meteors trained,
the volcanoes untamed,
the glaciers
sneaking up on my heals
with every tide.

now
I find myself

with no place
to hide.

one 07

say the words
until your skin
absorbs them;
until they are
the hum behind
the mechanism of thought
the truth that closes
your lips:

companion 07

you will be alone,
you will be alone,

I always knew
I'd be alone
at the end

you will be

of the world.

not,
soon enough.

a companion
in this
and all this
will fall aside
long lost longing,
a molted shell
it will sit
a shape echoed
beside me
from absence

and we will talk
with a vocabulary
and be one
of sad smiles
less
and glowing eyes
than alone

and being no one,
of all things
every one.

most of which
have never been,
for we are all alone,
for we are all alone,

and things
that so clumsily
for we are
were;
all al-
better
one.
for all of their
awkward physicality.

those stutterings,
those pointless putterings,

that made unknowing
survivable.

25

fly 07

my sheer and shimmer of wings
are caught upon the design
of another creature's making.
and the poetry of my pulse
is my limbs,
frantic and unfinding,
carrying
a shiver on every strand,
to that which will come
and swaddle me
in death.

its legs and mandibles
approaching,
my scent already
in its mouth.

then,
a wind,
a bluster,
the very luster
of the sun
and all days
before it,

my wings loosen

and I am free!

my flight
a multi-mirrored wind;
shivering and flying
close to the earth.
a heart beat fluttering
in a sustained
and organized fright
that defied fear
that gave Itself flight.
a vessel of blood vessels
transparent against the sun,
red strands entangling all the
lifeless to resuscitate
the never breathing
with the fracture

of its form and

former. leaving

a trail of fire
visible to only the cold
and every disturbed
molecule.

I dance as
upon every breeze,
a new pattern of me
weaves a new veil
through leaf & tree
so pointlessly

to the point
a pierce, a sting;

and I fly
faster.

a kaleidoscope
within my eye made more
radiant and varied
with flight and I
can smell sugar
from the flowers,
from the skin,
both living and dead,
but I am sated .

I fly
I fly
I
fly

into the red horizon
a slow dull drum
the distant sun
dimming.

the dream
of a cocooned fly.

sunrise 07

you turned pain
into wine

and sipped it slowly.

its cut
was a warm
upon all that
threatened
to stop cold,
as it slipped down
your throat,
passed all those
icy gears
and found your stomach,

inebriating all
the butterflies there,

wetting their wings
like a storm
and forcing them
to find shelter
elsewhere,
escaping
in your last sigh
upon possible things.

and in this breath
of nevers
and forevers,
you handed over
every flourish
of your face
as an instrument
to play upon.

the corners of your mouth
flickered smiles and frowns,
as both lived so close
together
upon the same curve
of lip.

your eyelashes
were dreams trying to
wake,
a waking
wanting a dream
as your eyes
slept, fitfully turning
beneath their blankets.

I watched you
without word.

such sounds were
clumsy limbs
in this dark,

so we waited
for sunrise.

the weak 07

you cried like that,
a cat cleaning there,
itself,
that's me,
your hands
stroking back mimicking
every misplaced hair. all the durable
every stray that endure
carefully found in your
a space gestures and words
to lay against the others in my eye;
until you
could open your eyes the darkness
and look up again; that snares light,

composed the retinal self,
compiled the holographic me,
and a
comfort this inner
that brings the outward
to everyone else; within

to me a skin
from the other side that loves
of me. with the shape
of its empty.
for those better parts
that could not
possibly

share my hands,
this skin,
that face
in the mirror.

i am not that strong.
i am not that strong.

i am the weak
what are you?

wilderness 07

now i understand.

i'm on the other side
of those eyes,
dull with pink,
gleaming at a razor.

i understand
that i never

understood.

no one can.

not without
the narcotic
of too much knowing.

how it fires off
the chemical potential
of every fear,

bullets expended
that leave only
holes, expanded
empties
that give birth
to echoes,
amplifying
this steady and pointless
heartbeat.

disallowing
even the peace
of silence.

that sound
is too strong to die
when it should.

its punctuation
should be my will,
the outer edges
of my hope.

but i am,
at least,
weeks passed
such borders.

in this wild,
in this wilderness.

this heart is a parasite
that uses me
as its legs,

and it must be
stopped.

to breathe 07

up from the dark,
an old,
now new,
with stark bones
and skin of
a lonely, distant train.

my head aches
from its sound,
on the inside,
pushing out
from my skull.

today was a bad day

to breathe.

I should have stopped
that last breath
and
the one that came after

but my lungs demanded
and I acquiesced,
from habit.

speaking
to non-existent company
to keep myself
practiced in words,
wanting ghosts to materialize
to scare all these
present ones away.

old relatives,
are you there?
have you been watching?
do you shake your head
at the madness I've become?

that the line of your blood
should have congealed
into such a person

as me.
or is there pity?

are your fingers
trying to stroke my hair;
a comfort I cannot feel.

or is all that I imagined
one mere lie,
one more one ended
conversation

that will just
keep me talking
for all the breaths
in between.

exhale 07

in this sitting,
this breath held
floating,
a bubble
growing,
against and within
bone;
a skin for a sun,
eyes for a light,

a leaf that will
uncurl

a flower opening
in splintered bloom,
that pollinates
a white wall
with crimson,

spreading me
exponentially
and microcosmically
into vapor,

an exhale.

as my lids close.

my fingers
fumble upon metal
and raise
its cold
perpendicular to my own.

bullet crack.

shot that shatters
the silences pressing
upon the windows
and sends them
scampering
for a hole
to hide in.

while I find one
to escape from

equilibrium 07

the sky.
its burning.

the ground is black
with night
with shadow;

and it is in me
standing
a single, vertical
point
against the horizon.

with my hands
upon my chest,
upon an opening,
with the wind
blowing through it.

this cold
its under my skin
and impossible to warm.

my arms surround me;
but I am
this

cold.

in this dark
there are things
faster than light.

the speed of terror.

it cuts the earth
at its diameter,
traversing fire
to find me.

my breath is
knocked from
my lungs
on impact
with this moment.

my mouth
is still snatching
for it back.

for all this air,
I cannot find it,

but stare
for the sun
(or a false one)
in this stagnant still
without, within
waiting for a break

in the equilibrium.

godless 07

a pulse free
splaying
and displaying,
a child spattering
her colors
upon the walls;

an ocean foam
filling;
a film
upon every nerve
to a flurry
of false firing
elevated passed thought;

but outside dogma.

until my skull
is a vessel
until my skin
is too taut
to be taught

anymore;

and this burgeoning
demands direct
exposure.

sun without heat,
earth without gravity,
pulse without a heart,

but remembering all these
in an
escaping echo
that has no sound
in a last laugh;

the godless
having no appointments
to keep.

33

good slave 07

a nodding lump
drowsing over a cup
of starbucks absinthe,

just an average
worn down anomaly
using stimulants
to stay

awake

and ideologies
to sleep.

running down networks,
rutting through,
plowing over,
a good little serf
in the new
feudal feud
billed each month
by the credit card company.

satisfied with my station
and them
with my stationary.

pro-life
anti-social
security

because good slaves
breed,
(go forth and multiply)

because good slaves
break,
(work the land)

because good slaves
don't retire.

good slaves die.

because the good
slave.

because only here
is young flesh
second
to old ego,

and tilled
into the soil;
good fodder
for bad fathers.

repeat 07

evil is ordinary
continuous,

the drone
in humanity's ear,

that we all
just got used to.

a machinery
that clicks away
heartbeats
in direct synch
with gloating smiles.

mass murder
is mass production
and bigotry,
the insane's quality control.

station 1
point a penis
rape.
repeat until docile.
station2
point a gun
fire.
repeat until quiet.
station 3
point to god
control.
repeat until asleep.
station 4
point a missile
if all else fails.
no repeats.

this universe,
this black ,
with no stars,
dimming
until cool
smooth and blended

and achieving
100% efficiency

pretty blue hell 07

glistening
at the edges of my shiver
of this shock,
of this nerve,
curled, congealed,
all too real;
an ice age begins
at the tip of each hair standing
and working in;
while another works
its way out
a planet core cooling

until they meet
where I will end

and leave
this pretty blue hell,

against the black,
just one more
spark
borrowing
its glow, its rain
its infinitely transient
calm
from sun and moon.

a self centered centrifugal
beautiful youth
ignoring ages passed and
coming
arrogant and immortal
like all its mortals

cheating life and death
with their mythologies
but right now
I get no fairy tale;

just the ending.

that
alone,

will keep my eyes
searching the dark
and my hands
clutching the white sheets
over my head,

until I drowse
and it seeks me

even there.

and in this cold
the snow is falling

and circling
is the wolf
that has been following

that shadow
upon the white
upon my periphery;
the apnea of my eye;

now it watches
without a growl

but with an appetite.

it knows I am done
and that
it will continue,

and so will
this pretty blue hell.

more weight 08
(for Giles Corey)

This horror
sitting on my heart,
this weakening beat
a struggle against it;
so it can stretch
to love,
to forgive,
to have the space
for anything…

but muscle pressed
to muscle,
there is
barely room
for this thinning
pulse of blood
unreaching
to my ever icing limbs
that I will have
to amputate
to save
this torso,
this brain,

this mind,
that will only
place one more
terrible weight
upon me.

with what it sees.
with what it

can not
will not

lie about.

stone by stone,

waiting

for my false confession.

that this is
god.
that this is
what god wants.

that this is.

then let all
this skin encases,
these ethereal reals,

go the way
of my flesh.
dissolve.
erode.

stone by stone.

better oblivion
than forever

with one more
megalomaniac.

and with
each heavy
judgment,

stone by stone

I say only
with my last breath.

"more weight."

ultraview 07

such strange travelers,
knowing their own minds,

only one isolated
second at a time.

a vapor trail;
a ghost behind them,
a black ahead,
upon which
such small
personal infinities
are projected.

an amnesiac
forgetting and foreboding
each step
across an unseen room

seeing

only their own feet

and still stepping.

I am but a breath;
a whisper, a word,
at an impossibly near
distance

against their ears,
speaking.

but
heard only by
the insane,
the sleeping,

and the awake.

emergence 07

pull this thread   that allow
and snap   all yesterdays
all the knots   to dangle
it creates;   and accumulate

pull it straight   catching
and empty   on all corners
all the loops   I might
it folds   walk around;

into   tightening
a single one   upon each
so all its entwined   muscle moved,
can hold   upon each
nothing   spasm of momentary more.

but   from birth,
one signal   to berth;
perpetuating
an impetuous   to this small me,
heartbeat,   to this small earth.

this flutter
that mutters
tomorrows
in my chest,

but not
these tangles
the wire-crossed
dug-in angles

that tie
me
to me;

untrue 07

I wanted to warm
myself against this sun

but only
managed the transience
of incandescence,
the occasional kindness
of civilization
that kept me

just inside
this light
enough.

the earth is
too round
to rest my feet upon,

the sky is
too blue
to not imagine it
black.

this flesh
too unmarred
to be unmutilated.

and all those perjuries
without juries
to articulated
to be
untrue.

this
is not

untrue.

all the horrors
we honor,
all the shrapnel
we give medals for.

all those
whispered
sweet little nothings,

that were
just that.

nothing.

all the cursing accusations
I spit
as
I splinter
in the hard moments;

are not enough
untrue

for me to love
or lie about them.

service 07

why am I

so hungry?

this growl
that grumbles,
an old man
to his slave
for his supper,

am I a servant
to all that
should serve me?

these functions
demanding
freedom, my will

and more so
to bend it
into whatever shape
survival demands.

to feed this skin
that feels too much,
this cold
that shakes
all words
from my teeth;
leaving only illiterate
consonants
to click there.

morse code for
more…more…more

do I really need
more?

or has this
flesh
developed a taste
for insatiability.

smaller 07

who are you
that cannot look away,
not from a truth
deliberately misquoted

in grey,
in black,
on paper,
in glow,

in this early dark
5am for all sleepers
and
the end for
the insomniacs.

but for you
the start of a bracing,
a muscle tightening,
pull up tissue and bone
into a braiding
of selective feeling;

a callous for
this protean skin of being,

that still
stared.

and with each
channel change
the shadow
on the wall changed

but the flame behind
still the same;

blue, cold
and dimming.

and your form
an eclipse between
casting a colorless contour
against it.

each image,
your eyelids pressed
upon slowly
with a gentle pressure
to hold that specimen
in place;
even as it
squirmed and fluttered
to escape observation.

for this
might be the last
of its kind

this one,
this unrepeated instant,

adding even its
miniscule meaning
to your accumulated,

and somehow you
felt smaller.

starting 07

she started.

it threatened to burst
this insulated sense
of separation.

this skin.

that held her in,
that held them out,
that held them
all

unbearably unmoved.

the her
that she kept
compact and creviced
in a corner
of this breathing husk.

it started

expanding
with missing,
with wanting,
that made it reach

a reproducing leaven
leaving her
with irrepressible life.

with edges pressing

against brittle bone
and all other borders
the world had for her.

it started
to seep from her eyes
it started
to clench her fists;

pressing her teeth
into a splintered grin

that kept her from
screaming.

it started.

and her fingers
fought
each point of rupture,
to smother
before another
would see

until she could
start
to shrink again.

semele 07

a barely
survived semele,
my eyes have
scorched my mind
with their seeing;

this conclusion
millenia
in the making.

the retinal rapture
that has
depopulated my countries,
silenced the streets
and emptied the beds
during the night.

leaving

only the shapes
of the missing
in wrinkled sheets
and ownerless shoes;

billions but
only one thought.
all the consciousnesses
I had
are gone

and the walls
can no longer
hold onto their echoes,
fading as paint
in too many suns.

as all
that is solid
erodes,

I am a sand
glittering
with infinite smalls.

can I reflect
brilliance without burning?

my mouth shapes
unarticulated awes
to name the gods
that do not exist,

but are all the same,

destroying us.

jovian 08

I closed my eyes
and made myself
a mirror.

your violence,
your lies,
twisted and floated
as jovian swirls
on the surface
of this bubble.

all the while
threatening me
with rupture,
with rapture,
the orgasm
in your god-upturned
lunatic eyes
as you imagine
all those
to be punished;

all those that
dare exist
and not be you.

my head swam
in this air
thinned by hollow words
that were the
concave shape

of all the empties
saying them.

I listened

instead, to the rain
each drop
a refraction
of each other,
of each another,
a subtle vibration

upon my skin a voice
in reflection
and sunlight;
an ethereal
from the mechanical.

and how this
unimagined
can imagine

beyond that window
a sliver, a slice
of moon.
an eclipse
passing slowly
with a single star as witness

beside pale blue.

a droplet
upon whose membrane
crawls specs
of spectacular illumination
that have only yet
to be enlightened;
to the dark,
to the sea,
a bioluminescent
which is the only
for fathoms of atoms
their conversations
eavesdropped upon
by a silence
a culmination
of all colors,
of all voices.

I drifted to sleep
dreaming of all the things

your god
tells me
I do not deserve.

judas 08

that smirk.
it curled upward
an obscenity

defying gravity,
defying flaw,
deifying cruelty

with your fat ruddy hands,
with your fat full belly,
with that flabby bulge
that made you male
and still managed
not to make you
a man.

but white
and ready for rape,
gave you
instant absolution
for all you may do.

for it was all
for their own good.

for it was all
for god.

defiling desperation
with that
IamsavedtheywillsufferIwillnot
thoseuppitycunts
thosefallenfaggots
thoseallthatdare
not
believe

me,
smile.

as you so lustfully
licked your lips
upon the possibility,
your eyes wandering
the sky
will false wonder.

not the blue,
not the clouds,
not the rain,
not the black beyond
speckled with stars,
infested with billions
of glowing galaxies
expanding outward.

not the blue
beyond the shore.

not the blue
that seduced a moon,
a moon that calmed
a sky, an ocean
into the blissful regularity
that allows life.

no.
you had no smile
for that.

only
that you
had made an insiders deal
with a kiss.

a judas.

unalone 08

this flesh
never fit me anyway,

and now
it's getting looser;
the sinew tie-downs
are unknotting
from bone;

the skin billowing
a white sheet
trying to imagine
how to be wind,

and how sun feels
when you swim
in glow
and refuse to go

through blue,
empty
but unalone.

a flutter
against a far,

getting nearer
but still
distant enough

to not
close the miles
between the hoped for
and the unknown

a haze, a shape
a horizon
dissolving
into foam of sky;

and stars heal
with cold air
clearing
all that is tearing

through black,
empty,
but unalone.

it lies 08

and there it lies,
insidious before my eyes,
that there is
no love on planet earth,

no matter how often we say
the word,
nor pronounce it with the most
believing
nor sweetest of tones.

no matter how our mouths
round upon it,
and how its syllables shape
our lips into a kiss,

it is not true
because we say it.
it is not true
because we believe it.
it is not true
because we do not live
it.

and there it lies.
and there it lies.

in this silence.
for minimum wage,
for social order,
for sex,
for ego,
for god;

3,000+ years and
this
is love?
no matter the ages.
no matter the age.

sold behind alleys,
sold behind laws,
sold before pulpits,
sold before birth,

and
told everyday after
quiet, blunt
but still heard,
it's just the way things are,
you are only a
well,

we all know the word.

but never say it,
how clean are your hands?

but it is the law,
no demands,
no supplies,

so say your Word,

and there it lies.
and there it lies.

No matter the pain,
No matter the loss,
No matter the cost,
No matter, not yours.

no matter, no matter
just behave.

love is not love,
if its only one inch
beneath you,

and
we are still

beneath you.

and this is not untrue
        because YOU say it,
and this is not untrue
        because YOU believe it.
it is true
        because WE live it.

beneath its lies.
beneath it lies.

in this silence
that privilege buys
no man will ever love
when one
woman is a slave.

and there it lies.

idontknow 08

a rabbit runs
before
my wheels,

pauses there
and I
pause upon it.

I am a prophet
awaiting direction
from patterns
of birds feeding
upon the lawn,
the scent of
an unseasonable rain,

but things are
always
as they were
and will happen
as they will.

(who's will?)
(who will?)

this intelligence
is
a superstition of self,
a personal myth
that ties
one moment
to another
and
builds synchronicities
into a
larger one.

should I take comfort
that this
sense of ending
may just be

my own,

a fashioning of fears fastening
onto one another
finding each fulcrum
on each unbonding electron.

and that this face
is nothing

more.

that this
haphazard happening
is one more
braid unraveling
into another.

that the self-righteous
are not right
but
only telling a self
a more intoxicating lie
to sleep at night
than wake to this

idontknow.
I don't know.

it hollows my bones,
the wind of it whistles
there
and is widened.

I hope I am wrong.
I hope I am mad.
I hope
that hope

is not just something
to hope
for.

I hope that

idontknow.

there 08

what was that,
just
there?

that voice
that tried to wake me
back
into the dream,

but the world
pulled me too soon

with its alarms,
its mechanical panics
all designed
to keep me

here.

there
had been a music
I know I may have been
dancing to

and faces welcoming,
trying to hold me

there

with their
smile,
with their
familiar unfamiliarity;
with their familial.

was it only a seduction
by strange creatures

or was it real;
real in wanting,
real in,
more real than

here.

had they poured another glass
to keep me
drunken,

their fingers holding fast
to my eyelashes,
knotting them
so a would not leave

there.

but the clock screamed
the coffee purred,
and
my aching side cried
under the weight
of its body.

their fingers slipped
and I slipped away

or to them
had I just disappeared?

or there
do I fill some skin always

there,

but both of us unremembering.

a flesh that grins
with no stopping edges,
a flesh that is not flesh
but
a glimmer,
a glamour

that is the true reflection

of this mind before
I open my eyes and go back

there.

parting 08

my pulse
is not worth
my life,

being
more than blood,
feeling
more than skin,

this throb of habit
that sustains
what inhabits,

though it may die
with both.

a traveler
from parts

it is more
me
than

unknown,

I'm

and someday
departing
into another

imparting.

unknown.

but while
here

it borrows breath
from wounded flesh

and sight
from eyes
squinting in the dim

of this dim
mention
of me,

a dementia
of machinery,
a mill
grinding a seed
of thought
into will,

veneer 08

I saw the veneer,
the hard skin
you slipped into
with such practice

that I barely
witnessed
the transition

between one you
and the next.

from that sigh
that held its own
skin

with a sense of ending,
with a desire for beginning,
for another

to feel this soft
as you did

in leaf,
in light,
in morning,
in the seconds

between
one breath
and
anot
her
's.

the precious
that cut inside
the most pink
and inner

that you held it
with empty arms
closer
and pressed it in.

part of you
would memorize
its shape
in yours.

and then

my foot fell
in the doorway,

your mouth closed,
yours arms folded,
you smiled, hard,
and
you blinked

like a street signal
for my next word.

gnarled geometries 08

this drive.

the rumble,
the wind,
the rewind,

the stops, the caution
the commotion of quiet
of what's coming,

the slight of hand
tomorrows,

slipping into another,

that I
indifferently
gaze upon.

the green
I try to find
precious
but only find
fading.

the infatuations
I need to cut away;

maybe I should be
truly alone

and depopulate
my mind

of these possibilities
that tease me
with their
impossible.

the liars get to love,

I do not.

the baboons get to believe
that there is no evolution,

and, unlike the gullible,
I get to grieve
with such hard edges

that I can see
all futures fall
into the black
beyond them.

all these blues,
all these greens,
all these truths,

made obscene
in the bare light.

all the suicides
the world
will murder me with;

why all those
I love you's
are meaningless
even when
you mean them.

especially then.

they are not going to
save me
from the gnarled geometries
shaping themselves
within my eyelids

I sit and watch
their angles surfacing
from
the void of this moment

becoming clear.

ugly 08

it hurts
too much

this outside,
this skin,

this malformed
shape
that holds
this inside

contorted.

this universe
twisted
by an inelegant
equation.

its measures,
distort;
its sums,
cut

me out.

that I must accept
this unacceptable,

that even
an optioned silence
will only attract
fingers

to make me
scream.

this passing
flesh,
passing

sagging inward
with its empty

asking with false pity,
demanding with stolen voices,
and
borrowed intellects,

raping
that which will not
open

and
murdering
that which does.

an ugliness
tolerated
everywhere

but in me.

such 08

such
an echo of a soul,
I keep coming
back to myself;

such a far away
me, to
such a hollow
now,

re
sounding
off the black
back
of my throat

forces up
to my eyes
the sun
I once saw

even in this rain.

and your voice
reminds
these cut out shapes

that they were once
wants

now only wanting

to at least see
such a world
filled
again.

and not
such an empty.

if only I was
a large enough
void
to swallow it

for you.

if only my death
can buy
such life,
and purchase
the attention of
such horrors

and put their eyes
upon me,
luring to rest
with me,

unspoken behind my lips.

all these
unfoldings
become again
creased and compact
quiets,

potential made impotent,
its unborn

taken back,
back
into
such darkness

so that
such greens,
such blues,

would have
no shadow
across them.

if only
there was a god

to grant me
such a prayer

and not
just all these voices
talking to themselves.

I have seen
such reds,
such glowing
as no generation has.

such pinks,
such browns,

such warmths,
touching with
such forevers

defying death
with
such knowledge of it.

and for all of it
to dim
is

too much.

is all there
left
to want,

that I could feel
such need

to make this
moment
such an infinity?

no more 08

there is not
a word
for what cuts me now,

just a reaction.

my neck is hardening,
muscles mustering
the will
that I cannot;

a jaw clenching,
biting upon
only itself,
and trying to do

no more.

a rage
I am trying
not to have,
a pain
I am condemned to;
I will be

no more

this neural
pattern of person,

that is more
that deserves no more,

that wants no more

screaming,
that only makes
those gloating smiles
wider.

a skin shuddering
at all the hands
without faces,
circling in shadow
to use it

to tear me
from me,
all the violations
I am told
I should be

thankful for.

no more.

the way 08

it's the way things are. . .

had niggers
swinging from trees
after they tried to vote.

had kikes
stacked and burned
for being.

had cunts
mercifully "loved"
by rule of thumb.

the way things are

words of those
committing atrocity

or just not
wanting to be woken
by it.

in this sea 08

the ocean filled
my nose,
a child's untrained
swimming.

I am
too immersed,
and
too unversed

for all these words
we have no sounds for
and cannot escape
for an open mouth
will drown
in this sea
and open eyes sting
with all the salt
in this seeing.

so my limbs and lungs
hold for those few
seconds
longer

for a rescue
that will only come

when I am floating.

inaudibles 08

she did not
speak
anymore

but simply
directed her eyes
to the next
possible silence

and walked
into it.

syllables had
become
too large,
too complex

for her
to shape
her lips
around them
anymore.

their edges
entangled

in the spiderous
connections,
now misfiring,

they flitted
there
in false flying.

she waited for them
to tire
for her
to encapsulate them
into something
more digestible

for those
pausing
for her to answer;

all those
asking how
she was,
explaining how
things were,

her role,
their god;
her place
they're god.

and
all the polite ways
she was to pretend

they weren't
saying it.

the prepackaged
that was expected.

she instead
allowed inaudibles
to blink her eyes
for all those
actually listening.

until tomorrow 08

isn't there something
I can put between
one second
and the next
so I can travel them.

something
that will not
dissolve
on contact
with light or air,

that is not a lie;
lying, relying
upon someone
else's
back
to endure
the steps I take
so casually,
so callously
across it,

or put me
beneath another's ?

one thing.
just one.
just one,

for now.

just
until tomorrow.

patina 08

your weathered face
has places
where it still shines.

there are
corners and crevices
where you hide yourself,
turquoise and black,
that remember
each drop of rain
and hold it to your skin

across time.

and press as close to me
as remembering.

glistening new,
where the wind has worn you;
listening raw,
to your own silence
as the eyes upon you
forget
when you were not so old
as you have become.

yet another never 08

her soul went all the way
down,
and through

traversing
hollow earth
one pole
to another.

a hole
in a skin
unseen
but covered
seemingly
separate,
but these seams
untied, tore
and could be seen

and stared
from her eyes,

as an ache
of being.

neither one
nor all
but between,
some directionless never
that was always there.

and with a flicker
of her lashes
she covered it,
shielding him
from what was behind
her eyes

for their shape,
would reshape
him
too, into this;
the want that would
always be wanting;

that tore
through
toward her
shaking the floor
from her feet.

and yet,

the rug stayed,
the chair was still,
the light bulb blinked.

her fingers stroked
across her lips

trying to re-teach them
how to conjure a kiss
from some unconscious
nowhere.

dark aurora 09

dark aurora,
there,
upon this blue,
this fear

that the sun
is sending
its light
everywhere

else.

for me,
its surrogates;

brown dwarfs
line streets,
pulsars
flicker their flat shapes
within my sleepless nights
upon my retina,
reversing the world.

this eye,
this iris,
constricting on a dark
ever
inward
in this light;

this nocturnal
blinded
by all brilliance.

I am trying
to see through
this moment
of self flagellation,
a world
of horrible constellation
in a sky
of numerous others,

all shining, infinitely,
down upon this tiny sphere
of me;

this temporary fluctuation,
in a temporal flash,
that knows
that this planet needs
to be knocked
from its orbit
or forever make
the same circle.

and a universe collapses
into a solipsism,
ranting to itself a soliloquy
of computational error
that can have more

than one solution;
all of which solve
nothing,

but keep me calculating
until I dissolve

in this grass
growing, dying;
with these stars
that will die too,
but at a different scale.

and between
these measures,
my miniscule resolve
finds a map
in a small meandering line
of a crack in a concrete wall,

because it is the only shape
that doesn't remind me

of all others.

Galileo 08

I am Galileo
and his telescope.

an eye
both mind
and instrument,
piercing through
dense atmospheres
into a world
only hinted upon
in hazy spheres,
rising to my gaze
from their long,
now discovered,
now enlightened,
dark.

but still

in the same
distant cold.

the light
of their sun,
creases
and caresses
their indifferent
faces

but
I know.
but
I saw.

places
where I will
never set foot,
but have taken
the first steps
toward,

this mind
destined for dust
on a small earth,
as my footprints
reshape
the remnants
of those before.

those
that knew,
those
that saw,

so I could see

and all that follow
could see
more.

destinations 08

I have grown
beyond this flesh,

and now
this skin
that protected
such soft pink,
now
tightens and twists
me
into the shape
of all

its hungers,
its desperations,
the harms
that can be-
        fall it.

its cuts
bleed me,
this present,

its scars
numb me,
this memory

and
its mortality
condemns
this real,
this ethereal,
all these
growing
under such
a small sun,

to a shared death,
in the same dirt,

but to different
destinations.

horizon 09

i am pressed thin
between
sea and sky

spreading flat
as a horizon

line,

because
the depths of
the ocean
drowns

and i have not
the capacity
to fly.

i spit out
sun
and swallow
moon,

squeezing
it through
my narrows,
passed
the hard
in my throat;

a division
that is
border
of all worlds

necessary
but itself
undetectable,
forever distanced
no matter
how many steps

you take
toward me.

from me 09

in this fog
somehow
my words
find clarity.
the crisp edge
of a train-bell,
of a grumbling engine,
of a rain soaked street
hissing;
even as
the street lamps
created their own
haze
and tree limbs
look as
black smoke
rising from their roots,
each a
slow smoldering.
my mind
cuts
into the next
moment,
using all its doubts
as a new form
of certainty
of now.

behind me
dissolves,
yellow lines
and whole neighborhoods

as new ones
coalesce
from formless gray.

this me
travels
into the
next me
seamlessly
performing
all its
hello's and goodbye's
with each ,
unearned,
yet still
existent being.

mercifully
clouding
all
pasts and futures
from me.

found 09

how did i find you?
a camouflaged consciousness
hiding
in the tall leaves
of this jungle;
your eyes gleaming
out
with a
fearing fascination
upon the rest;
as an animal
displaced
from its habitat,
ever
learning another.

first
i felt you,
turning up each hair
upon my skin
as a wind's
orchestration
in tall grasses;

and in turning
upon such
breezes
catching your scent
secreting
behind spring flowers,

i heard
your pragmatic
panic
scatter leaves
and push back
branches

until you
found a shade
from which
to spy.

but i followed
the light
in your gaze,
the blinking beacon,
that seemed
to guide
the pace
of my approach,
and
knelt waiting

as you
crept out,
your disguises
marking each
passing inch
of what you saw
in me

until
each reflex
relaxed,
unreflecting,
and

i found you.

pull 09

I close my eyes
and

pull

the black in,
close as blanket,
warm as womb,

the outer edges
of a cosmos
collapsing,
as this one
does
from within.

while
all these
ever so rational voices
try to

pull

me out.
with extortions
of affection,

we want what's right
for you...

pull

yourself together...
we only want...

their want,
each a tearing finger

pull

ing

back my privacy

with pills,
with fists,
with loving hands,
pleading
for my life, to

pull

me from this,
this flesh born,
and deemed
only for raping,

this mind
threatened
into silence,
pursuing a truth
no human can have,

pull
ing

threads it knows
will
only unravel,

and I will
no longer
be

able
to be

a consumer,
a consumed,
or
in consummation

with anything
around me,

I pull
in.

near 09

you slept
nuzzled to my neck
and with a
sharp breath
you woke,
you realized
how near you were
to me.

your eyes
searched about
for a topic to converse
about
to play down
the moment
while your legs,
while your arms,
crept
to increase
our distance,

but did it
so slowly
as to be
below
my noticing,

so as to not
convey
revulsion.

but could i
not be more aware
of your every
motion

when in
your stillness,
your proximity
had held me
from any sudden
movement

so I would
not
wake you.

it was
as if I had
stumbled upon
some wild creature
sleeping
in its den,

and careless
stepped
upon a crying branch.

then all at once
you woke
eyes glowing
calculating
both
your curiosity
and
how far
a single leap
could take you.

69

feasting 09

a flower
open upon a sun,

your eyes
open upon my face,

a rose
its mouth,
feeding on
a given radiance,

your mouth,
feeding on
a promise
I never made,

but got
bouquets for.

and I open.

even when my eyes
are too tired to.

your flesh
feasts on mine,

while my eyes
(you barely notice)
are watching
each petal
fan out,
silken receptors
to a star.
its small appetite
suckling
on a million year
mother,
forever offering
to any.

while you
attempt to extract
milk from stone.

I envy
those two;
their distance,
and
their intimacy,

you lie
back
sated, sleeping,

and never
once
said my name.

2012 09

the air
it made my heart
shiver.

its fingers
electric to this flesh
lending
a sheer,
a shimmer;.

its dead nerves
simmer
and jump
their ecstatic panic
threading
into a new skin

skein,
tethering each end
to new stars
as the planet
shifted
beneath my feet.
its tectonics
fracturing and refitting
toward
the gravity
of a different sun,

the scattered
surviving species
from their caves,
cautiously
resurface
to this
new surface,

their feet
less sure
of their position
on earth

and even less
certain
of the sky

with
its forever,
its blue
that held
the black at bay,

the world had ended.
but still continued.

and all that
had been cataclysm,
had been a mere cough
to a sphere
throwing off
the tickle
of tiny terrorisms

that just happened
to grow
there
while it was sleeping.

and I shivered
again.

and smiled.

surely redeemable 09

her eyes
upon me
still;
an exhaustion
passed sleeping.

her breaths,
a carefully regulated
patience,
she
was barely

having

with me,
with my words,
that surely
we
(that ever inclusive
yet
exclusive 'we')
as a race,
as a kind,
had managed
for millennia,
that somehow

we
must be
surely redeemable.

she stared.

her breaths,
her breadths,
rebutting me
with their unmoving,

all expounding
on the

Cinderella slipper
she had inherited
though her feet
too big for,

it was either
bind, bleed or break
or
go barefoot

for a prince
that never actually
was.

the hands
she could
still feel
claimed a piece
of her flesh,

and the respective
piece of mind
tethered to that tissue
by a twisting
all-too-feeling nerve

leaving her
a phantom limb
to all her
selves surrendered.

even now
the ache was amputated.

"surely…"
she said.
her whisper,
a seismic fissure
splitting her face
with a smile

that rattled
the china,
the dusty knickknacks,
and all else
not nailed down,

and shook
all my certainties
away,
before sinking
behind a blink
that held one
of those breaths
like it was
the last friend
she had.

my lips
tried to form
new words,
but were too practiced in
old excuses;

and she
looked up.
"redeemable,

kind of like
a coupon
for something
you don't want
anyway…"

not a deal,
not even useful,

just taking up space
because you cant
throw it away.

she smiled.
"surely"

careful 09

your answers
were careful,

and that
enraged me;

the way that
when
I sought,
or pursued
you,

you looked long
at me
as if
slowly translating
a child's
mispronounced jabber
into words
you could answer.

and I
wanted
answers,

but
only got
responses.

"why did you..."
received a sigh
and tightened lips,

"why didn't you.."
opened those lips,
your eyes
rising flares
that just as suddenly
sunk,
dimming,
down...

and then
I would stab
with the sharpest blade
in my arsenal,
just to make you
cry out,

"did you EVER love me?..."

and it would only
cut me;

the way you
looked up at me,
a patient from
a coma
just realizing the years,

it wasn't hate,
and that
was why
it hurt,

you knew
what you wanted
to say,
but you knew
you couldn't say it
unless
you knew
it was true.

we knew
each others lies
to well for that.

we both felt
the seconds stretch
taut
around your hesitation,

as you tried
to resuscitate
a light in your eyes,
a pulse to push
the syllables out

and answer me.

because time,
because doubt,
because even back then,

we both
had been more
running away from ache,

than toward
each other.

the debris
from that collision
was just now
settling,

and it was time
to assess the damage.

"of course"
you lied,
unsure if
you lied,

but said
a truth
anyway.

that you
a least
cared enough

to be careful
with me.

excercism 09

the fury
was waiting;

sitting,
barely patient,
in the backseat;
clicking
its ravenous black
fingernails
on the back
of her skull,

with the same word
wincing with
each impact,

when?

you know when.

she felt its eyes
narrow
in contempt
to ensnare her
between
the thick lashes,
its mouth pouting,

an undiverted adolescent
began to rant,

I'm hungry
her stomach growled.
I'm tired
she yawned,
This car is old and noisy
she sighed.
you should get a new one.
she bit her lip.
Why don't you?

you know why....

it smirked
at the tender tissue
it had stumbled upon,
and how
it always worked
every time

why....
you know......
I don't .....
it licked its sharpened grin
explain it to me....

because I don't have
the money

why
her mind became
an overstuffed pincushion
with all this needling.

because
where I was
born from,
born to,
born as,
born beneath,

born apart

and all the other
demographics
that had decided,
that the chosen
pretended
were choices.

this life
was not hers.
she was
its foster mother,
adopting the results
of another's abuses,

its folded arms
and cold staring
daring her
to punish it.

she parked
the car,
a single set
of footsteps
found their regular path
to a beat-up locker.

she changed,

in the mirror
staring down
a body
she didn't want

and a brat's revulsion
...god you're ugly...

she ignored
it's regular instigation.

that wasn't why
she was
there.

her well worn
sneakers
found the tread mill,

and began
a journey of many steps

all in one place
kind of a metaphor
for
your life
it mocked,

legs moved faster,
a little hamster
in her wheel
and faster
run away, you coward...
faster,
faster,
faster,
until its words were winded

and her pores
were a million mouths
screaming,

in a way
that she couldn't,

and some neural panic
gave her
a legal dose
of oblivion.

unfolding 09

and I am trying
to think
of anything

else
at this moment.

my every forgiveness
has been ungiving.
my every patience,
a delay to buy
my docility.

when I see,
too simultaneously,
that I will live,
that I will die,
and I will spend
at least
a little
of each day,
in elaborate labors
to undo,
or just keep to myself,

what has been done
to me.

I can't look at it.
not right now.
not right now.
not right...

now,
my eyes gradually
focus
upon what my retina
has registered,
but my mind has not,
staring through
this thought.

a single drop
shivering,
refracting,
the most vibrant pink
and a sun
that will eventually
evaporate it.

it balances
on the downward curve,
magnifying
the deep magenta
vein beneath,
that bleeds
into so many others,

on a soft
that shames silken,
that makes all else
brief, bereft, and brittle,

when it
is the most
easily bruised
of all,

a rose.
its petals
half splayed
but still
coyly coiled.

it bobs
in the breeze,
its stem stringing
to earth,
a just-lost balloon
that has yet
thought of sky.

its outer edges,
ridged by feeding aphids,
its inner,
a pucker
of pursing complicates,
the design
of its process of
unfolding;

the sun,
the cold,
it's blossoms
and near –witherings.

I know its color,
I know its scent,
I know its structure,
and all their
purposes.

browning at season's end
or
freed by a wind
into a swarm
of coral butterflies.

I know its end.

but I can't help
but wonder,
if a flower
ever
sees itself?

suicide by pen 09

the wheel
of my silver Nissan
trembles
in my hands
as my foot forces it
down
the poorly repaved
route 3 north
at 80 mph,

into the cotton pink sky
that some careless child
has lit a match to;

so beautifully burning.

I imagine Boston's
jagged silhouette
against it,
a child's frantic cutting
through a watercolor.

the misaligned axle
registers each upraised
lump,
thump,
of callously dumped
tar,

or the canyon left
when the road is ripped
away
by friction heated radials.

these rhythms
tap telegraph
to my temporal
lobe,
lobbing
syllables
that crash

particles in a collider,
spitting,
spiraling out
fully-formed words

that jump
from my tongue,
a springing vibrato,
ecstatic children
from a diving board
at a public pool,
shrieking,
belly-flopping,
or
flapping like
fish without water,
my words
without paper,
and will die
on the deck
or dive back
into the sea.

my hand excavates
the landfill
of my purse,
its piled strata,
a record
of perpetual
over-preparedness,
that always
leaves me searching.

my eyes
delegate
to my fingers
a task they are
ill equipped for,
their fat five
blindly digging moles
whose only progress

is disarray.

then
my eyes stray

from the road

to the bottom,

the singularity
down which
every writing utensil
I have
disappears.

my hand
reaches deep
into the black.

THUMP

the pavement
sends the car veering,
I still search
my hand steering

I can see it...

THUMP

my brain
turns my wheel arm
back
and my tires start
grinding,
my fingers
finally finding....

damn, it's caught...

THUMP

I turn again,
avoiding exploding tires,
visualizing
the hot rubber
spattering
on the road,

I've turned too
far.

a screaming horn,
a mutely raging driver,
shakes his fist,
contorts his face
behind a window,

the sound,
and the rush
of my own blood,
scorch
all signals
from my mind,

and I am
only hearing
my own heartbeat.

I'm getting a recorder...

savor 09

sweating out
a wine,
I am the cask
it has aged in
and with
time and solitude

I have become
dryly sweet.

my words,
my silences,
the result
of years
of ferment,
foment
of my brief moment
beneath the
firmament
of all the arches
built so solidly
over me.

out from the
dark cellar,
I leave my thoughts
having long become
whispers in the corner
pointing upon me
with
ridicule and awe,

at this thing
growing
in their presence,
these musings
amused
at their muse,
at their maker,

either children
fleshly fresh,
absent minded
lunatics
running from one room
to the next
yelling their
non-sense taunts,
in their hide and seek
haunts

or ancient
slow-linking,
sharp-eyed,
well-rehearsed
criticisms
that crack
and fall
from wrinkled lips
as fractured glaciers,
splashing
into my blood stream
to cool me
into cowardice.

their chants
the same.

"you should,
you should have..."

but now
in this sun,
my foot twitches away
their clinging fingers,
pulling upon my toes
like hungry birds.

I sip slowly
the sunshine,
a fine port,
and let it be
a sea
between
every neuron.

for these doubts
cannot swim,
let them drown.

I will choose
to be intoxicated
with summer,
a three month
respite.
my feet curling
in the sand,
keeping my worries
as mere tourists

that I nod to
then let pass.

I have all winter
to be snowed in.

really? 09

"I like being a man..."

really?

what is that
supposed to mean
really?

and my teeth
wanted to rip away
the callous of
your rationalization,

but instead
ground
upon the realization,

about what
you were
really
saying and how
you expected me
to let you get away
with it.

that smile
that gloated,
the eyes
that floated
so above all the things
that would never touch you,

all side-benefits
and default privileges
of having
a white dick.

and how
all the
enabling little stepfords

with their batting eyes
adored you,
"he has such traditional values"

and how
I shouldn't be

so unreasonable,
after all wasn't i
really
being sexist?

it's that pms.
its that liberal bias media.

what?
really?

my rage wasn't just
at the idiocy,

but how
you never had
to know
what never
feels like.

not really.

a disparaging whisper
from a magazine cover.

a career counselor assessment.

hanging
in hymns about apples
in lemming cathedrals.

a hand at your throat
enjoying your struggle.

fingers reaching
deep, low
and playing you
for the cries
you will let out,
licking into your ear
about your shallow grave.

a smug
in a black smock
deliberating
on how much
a rapist owns your days.

you know,
all the things
that decided our lives

really.

and you,
sad-eyed,
mewed
while sizing up
the pickings
of these clucking hens
for your mattress,

about what happened to family,
about how you've be made
        to feel guilty
        for being born

the wrong sex.

what?
REALLY?

funeral 09

I blow on the
hot
black coffee
while words
from the podium
grind
the ground
from beneath
me,
a foundation
I thought sunk
so deep
that the earth
had long coiled
gripping to them
muscular
the legs
of an enraptured
woman,

she was,
she is,

refusing to release

but I am
not necessary
to this earth,

I always know it,

but having it
thrust
so deeply
to my attention,

the old coffee
seemed sweet
against
this bitterness,

I swallow it
steaming,
boiling,
it creates
the mirage
of a smile
upon my face

in distorted
convulsive waves
as if off
of desert rocks.

I am alive

and for some reason
that is not enough,

and for some reason,
it is too much,

that the life
that had just passed

was
mid-action,
mid-being,

its ripples
just beginning
to touch
some outer shore

while mine
merely sway
against porcelain,

the result
of my shaking hand.

you tried 09

you said once
to me;
ok,
more than once.
many, many more times than that,

"who ever said life was fair?"

it was a phrase reserved
for all those special occasions,

the hard chores
a child never wants to do,
the hard people
a child would rather not meet,

or just
when you wanted me
to shut-up
in the only way
your constant raging could.

and that way
you could pretend,
you were teaching
me something.

well, you weren't.
well, you were...

you tried to teach me
that my anger had
no right,
no power,

beyond
the tiny clenched,
white-knuckled fists
that held it at the end
of my arms

and going no further.

at first,
because I was
small and helpless,
an then
from all those
small and helpless
before me.

you tried to teach me
that my desire had
no place,
no reality

other than
the poster pasted walls
I hid it in
feeding it
as a wounded starling

and wanted no more

at first
because it was
the only life
and later
because
it was
any life.

the years were full
of such lessons,
all by rote, overwritten,
ever-repeating;
and all the substitutes
and stand ins
that would fill in for you,
somehow finding me
in every attempted truancy

you tried to teach me
in the only way
that failure could,

by being human.

maybe, just maybe 09

your face avoided
me
with the expectation
that I pursue
and

maybe,
just maybe,
be the one worthy
of you.

I was supposed
to seek you out,
follow
through dark
and narrow,
twisted time

into your black egg
and rot there
in hope
that

maybe,
just maybe,
you might come out

of your fragile shell
of fracture.

well, sorry.

maybe,
just maybe,

I was a little
too trapped
in mine.

maybe
all those
unanswered
phone calls
were just

me
too overpopulated
with voices
already
in this skin,

to let yours
in.

maybe
while you bathed
in breaking,
I was
getting out
the dustpan,
collecting
from black soot
corners,
all the dead skin
of old me,
sifting from this dust
scattered old seconds,

for any piece
I could find.

maybe,
just maybe,

my breast
had no milk
left
for you to suckle,

my ears
too thick
with your waxing
upon
your alone,
your unheard,
your tapping tympanic
tell-all self-bio
that always managed
to find a tympani
to play upon,

my throat
too tightened
with all the coming
practical terrors
that could
not measure,
to your
abstract abandonings.

maybe
I just couldn't,

maybe
I just wouldn't

and
maybe,
just maybe
I shouldn't

have to.

secrets 09

I kept you
as a secret,

pursed
behind my lips
for all I wanted
to tell,

but every face
that I knew,
would only disapprove.

so instead
I kept
silently reciting
every detail
and
embellishing
every open end

into all its
alternate possibilities.

all the ways
I might see you
again,
all the ways
you might just
see me.

practicing
comedies, tragedies

dangling
upon my lip
as a teasing kiss
that I hesitated
to consummate,

I kept it,
in that ever before

levitating between
ache and relief,

as starving
but only feasting
upon aromas,

and not the meal.

until I am so close
I feel your smile
rather than see it,
patiently waiting.

and the eyes
I dare not look into,
warming around me
as your arms anticipate.

until this distance
can no longer be
kept

and I plunge in
folding your lips in
and then apart
petal outward,
and the nerves
pressing up
through pink,
reach as hands
to their corresponding
in yours,

their fingers
enfold and lock
us together.

and the only
range of motion
we have is
ever inward,
searching behind
each others smile

for those kept
secrets.

cocoon 09

we spent all day
rolling
in a cocoon
of our own skin,

pushing against
it
but attempting
no escape.

you fed
on my breasts,
a child kissing
on whipped cream.

my fingers curled
in the strands
of your hair
in half-lidded
awe
of a texture
they must touch
and ever
reconceive.

we warmed
our cold,
with proximity,

while every extremity,
curled as caterpillars,
upon each others
complementary
close,
inner ,
contours.

and we decided
to not become spring
just yet,

but stay blanketed
in this winter.

low place 09

and there
in the crinkling page
as old fire,
are higher words
than mine.

they sit
as pressed leaves
between the covers,
each still
carrying with them
the sonorous echo
of their former life.

the smell
of day
plucked away
from a living tree
in a summer's meandering,
ever forward,
just then unfolding,

and held
by a warm hand
to the lips,
breathing in
the earth,
the rain,
the sky,
the sun,
memorized
in its intricate
inner veins,
all the hours
recalled
and
forgotten
there;
green and glistening,

waiting
as a bookmark
for the next
curious eye.

holding a last sigh,
exhaled
upon opening
and borrowed
in another's breath

with its own words
that all come
from the same
low place.

always 09

these lines
span my
hemispheres,
the tectonics
of my shifting,
of the directions
that gravity
has pulled
that sun,
that moon,
that centrifugal
dizzying spin,
that

always
had me

looking in all ways
than at myself.

it was fall into the sun
or fall away
a cold starless planet.

well, that was
always
the threat,
since the highest
of authorities
have rewritten
and at always their
discretion,
constantly revise
what is natural,

as if anything was ever,
as if anything was ever
not,

these nevers
and always
somehow happened
anyway,

in all these fictional
absolutes,

the Cinderellas,
the Humpty-Dumptys
the fairies
that took my teeth
when I was asleep,

and upon waking
found a few coins
on the pillow
for all my trouble.

I should have known
then
that this was a cycle
that would
always
be expected of me.

that each night
a lie balmed realization,
each dawn
a socially expected amnesia

from all those
who claim the horizon
and therefore
all my
yesterdays and tomorrows.
all my always…
some part of me
always
illuminated,

and always
show me
that I am
the sole source
of my revolutions.

anyplace else 09

on this morning
I listen to the soft falls
of my footsteps
on the creaking floor,

wishing I was
anyplace else
from this room,
from the earth,
from myself.

anyplace,
anyplace else...

and my feet
then
shuffle faster.

all the digital
flickering and fluttering
turned off long ago
because, for all that noise,
I finally know

the world and I
have no words
left;
not for ourselves,
not for each other,

but I look
for them anyway,
in the wallpaper,
in the ceiling,
in some untouched
crease
of me.
are they
anyplace else?

all solid syllables
have been
masticated
and masturbated
upon,
regurgitated
to make
their texture,
their taste,
easier to swallow
a ground up
medication
stirred into
a pudding cup.

the old words
turned musty
in yellowing paperbacks
that were once
caressed in beds
accompanied on buses,
rounding,
pronouncing,
the private human world
in sensual serif,
hooking one
to another
through
borrowed pages,
bringing
anyplace else,
anyplace you were,

these utterances
are now trapped
behind the tight lips
of the mad,

occasionally
escaping
in fits and sputters
of seemingly
moronic mutterings;

over coffee cups
allowing passage
and apologetics
for your sparse
change
while you look
anyplace else,

down halls
of mental wards
murmuring
of daddies and uncles
and medicine cups
while you talk of
anyone else,

in front of the TV
blinking at the blasphemy
of so-called reality
and twitching
trigger fingers
at tire blowouts
reminding them of
someplace else,

those spirants
are long spirits,
ghosts that our
dogma and disbelief
have made disappear.

and who listens
to them anyway,

when its so easy
to drown it out,
when it is so easy
to be

anyplace else.

I watched you 09

I watched you
when you thought.

when you thought

no one was looking.

casually retracing
the, even now,
fluctuating features
of a human face
made even more
human
by its
malleable malformed.
the lines around
your eyes
counted out the years
in the steady flow
of currents,
all the rivers
of past epochs,
now dry deep
canyons
waiting for the next rain.

and then others
entered
unintentionally
fracturing
the silence
we so familiarly
and easily
had with each other.

and you welcomed it.

I watched,
as
you watched,
your glance
alighting upon
each passing
expression,
a flutter of fascination,
flitting among flowers
collecting from each
inwardly curled whorl
and opening them
up to sun
in an outstretched
smile.

I watched you
as
you watched,

a mirror
lending its
reflected light
to anyone
before you.

hard 09

and it is hard
this softness
that lets even
the vague memory
of you
press so deep
into my flesh
that it bruises,

coloring my
pale skin,
a plum plover
eggshell
shattering
and resealing
itself
with each impact.

but the shapes
there
are not your fingers.
there are no
telltale
configurations
of ovals
grasping
upon my neck,
upon my arms
in some violent
possessive
shaking.

no.
your hands never
touched me.

nor
are they
the hard
treaded mandala
of a sneaker,
a boot,
or even
your bare calloused
foot,

for you never
kicked me,

even when I was
down,
a coiled fetus
crying to herself
because she
could not curl
so completely
inward

as to disappear.

no.
these marks
are from
all the ways
I have pressed
into
the hard
of your absence.

pulse 09

this pulse,
it is running
the rapids,
the rabids
coursing my arteries,
stiffening my neck
with their currents
forcing my face
upward into the wind
for a cold reprieve
to sober me
of these thoughts,
but instead pulls
my lips back,
my teeth outward,
and
I taste the blood
around me.

all of history's
thrashings leave
countless volumes
of hemoglobin
atomized into the air
along with Caesar's
last exhale,
spinning with the world
in an ever circle
along with these
old schools of fish
matriculated in matricides,
the mothers
that a fictional father
inseminates
with a well crafted insanity.

all of it looping
like a lunatics
pacing,
retracing
steps and not
a spiral staircase
upward.

those helixes
are locked in cells
of these enslaving
shaven monkeys
and only climbed
in a dictated evolution,
passed
from one grasping
opposable hand
to another,

to one more
pulse.

the next germination
of beating hearts
whose veins will
bleed,
whose knees will
kneel,
whose backs will
bend
but
whose voice will
not be more
than a vapor
circulated,
condensed
then precipitated
in the next
rainstorm,

which will precipitate
another.

I feel it in my pulse,

all these past beatings,
pushing upagainst mine,

set and mistimed
to their
inherited rhythm.

mirror II 09

I do not
think
of myself.

instead
I run quickly
by mirrors
after a shower,
by windows
on the street,

and only smile
nervously, politely
when forced into
inescapable acquaintance
with them
(or any of their other)
much as all those
nameless relatives
at all those reunions,
counterfeiting affection
as a counter defense.

and when I can,
I look down.
look,
those are my feet,
always trying to out-step
themselves.

anything,
to not think
of myself,

but I'm lured back
eventually,

not a self-seduced narcissus
bending to its own beauty,

but a tsunami survivor
crawling out,

permeated and pummeled
and taking account
of the carnage,

of the years that happened,
of the moments that didn't,

no
I really try not to think...

no no no
not now

think about halfway around the world,
starving.

think about 2 feet away,
wanting.

think of things to do,
think of things to think,
think of maybes,

but never
think
of nevers,

those will grind your teeth
and
bend your bones
with the weight of all those

words
written in another's
judgmental glare,

just stare

away.

it is simply easier
to not think
of myself.

constant 09

and it is
my constant companion,

white knuckled
it clutched
my books
in a schoolyard,

watching
all the other legs run,
all the other mouths squeal.

its eyes gleamed
with mine
from a backseat,
black with night
and an angry
parental silence,

gazing
at all the golden windows,
at all the other lights.

it sat with me
doodling
ignored warnings in
subliminal signals
on college ruled lines.

it sang with me
in a four walled
sanctum,
sound and soul-
proofed,
so I could hear
my voice.

it was behind
the wheel;
humming, laughing,
screaming and
flipping the finger
to all those
distracted drivers
that cut me off.

it has never lied,
even as its hands
have always
hurt me.

at least,
it has never lied.

across my universe 09

on Feb. 4 2008
at 7 pm,
at 186,000 mps,
toward Polaris,
our axis star,

a voice flowered
outward
transmitted from
deep space antennas,
singing about
fluttering wind
in letterboxes,
of broken light
and
loving suns
and how

nothing
is going to change
my world.

the brittle tones
crack upon their own
accidentally spoken
realizations,
that 29 years later,
already broken
but somehow
still speaking,

finding an inertia
in the void,
and maybe
a destination.

and I can not help
but in all my
silly sincerities
and
childish maturities,

to hope
that somehow
they will
with bounding leaps
overtake and outrun
the first television
transmission,

an angry little boy
with a crooked cross,
and too many
straight-legged
followers,

that somehow,
John,
even in echo,
will out-charisma
Hitler.

that humor and love
travel lighter,
even faster than light

and an equal
lucidity
will answer back,

across the universe,

with its
own foresight,
feeling and
foolish frailty.

but by then
something,
most certainly
something,

would have changed
my world.

just like being there 09

I watched you
in the dark,

the world flickered
before us
in hi-def
but undefined.

every pore
carefully articulated,
the result
of numerous
research teams
manning long hours
in laboratories

so that
these shapes
would be more real,

just like being there.

while we sat,
well fed
and ruminating
our snacks,
our digital zoos
spring to life
in the every hours

and with each
fluttering photon
struggling against
the screen
as an entranced moth

came the words,
came the numbers,
came the faces,

all traveling
the circle of this
small blue droplet,

that suddenly
became
more small,
more breakable
with each
new broadcast.

in the glow,
your eyes
began to glisten,
your lips
balanced
clumsily against
themselves
and
your throat
twitched with some
captured creature.

I lifted the remote
to give you mercy
in darkness.

but there was no
disconnecting.

for you,
just knowing was

just like
being there.

photon 09

from the night
starlight falls
though the suns
stay pasted to the black,
their millions ago
find me
millions later
in a conversation
that must be
eternally
one sided,
always with
the remembered
or
the imagined,

the only witness,
a single photon
shimmering, simmering
on the surface
of my eye,
reaching back
into my retina
bending in worship
to its apse

and then spiraling
down
a nerve
to find
a synapse
and there
it will explode
outward
onto
all the others.
disentangling
every knot
knitted
by expectant fingers,
and
disappointed silences,

illuminating, white
as a passing comet
to all my primitives
and their
primordial awes,

flickering light bulbs
in all my childhood
hiding places,
forcing them out to play.

until the particle
travels back
passing all my
higher functions,
even my lower ones,
to my amygdalae,
the two dangling
inner eyes
of my emotional brain,

the place of scars
and badly set broken bones,
recorded in
my well rehearsed
worries and fears,

there the photon
glows,
its light
sears the sight
of all my
by-rote reflexes,
untried terrors
and blind allegiances,

until there is
only light

and only me

to see it.

snap out of it 09

the sky is ice
that the trees
shatter.
their black grip
tearing at the blue-gray
for the sun
they know is there.

they can feel it,
their tough bark,
in this season,
is more tender tinder
than mine
and burns
just at the thought
of summer,

though I seemed
to have forgotten it.

I tried not to,
attempting to
store it in the caches
of my own flesh
but my skin
does not blush brown
only red,
at the mere suggestion.

on sweltering days
I drank it deep
into my bone marrow
and sealed it
with spicy food
and sweet wine,
but the wind
cooled it
like the coffee
in my cup.

without
that internal warmth
my limbs are
growing heavy
with
growing icicles
that crack
along with the
glaciered ground
at every step.

even my voice
us a struggling starling,
it feet tangled in thorns,
all those
old hesitations,
visitations
frozen interlocked
by all those old blames.

it squawks.
as my muttering miseries
fly out
condense in the cold air
ice there,
then fall.

and the ground
crackles again

my foot
finding the shards
and then
finding that gravity
is a capricious constant,

as my foot slips,
the earth spins
off its axis
and swings back up
into my back,

a cold hand
knocking some sense
into me,

a slam down,
my voice thrown out,
but another in my mind,
my mother,

"Snap out of it girl!"

I lay there,
and the world
falls back into place
and my breath
slowly slinks
back into its
burrow,

my snarling snares
let loose
and the starling
slips
free,

ascending
as its own flock,

the sound
against the hard sky

of my own
laughter.

darling beloved 09

"my darling beloved…"
her teeth grinds
on the words
"his sister knows"
sisters always know,
they are the first to find out
about brothers,

when they aren't
holding the memories
to their mammary
milking the past
because the present
is dry and needs to be
reconstituted.

"he's doing it again…"

I assume
he's trying to fix
something again,
something digital, delicate
and therefore disagreeable
when his
thick, calloused hands
only know the
gears and cogs
they learned upon,

you know, those things
you can slap back into shape,
a technique that is less effective
with those new flickering faces
that shut down
as stubborn adolescents
when treated
too roughly.

he's drunk
and pounding the keyboard,

a monkey at a typewriter.

I don't think that even given
forever,
he will ever
write Hamlet.

instead the screen
stutters and gasps
in texts to match
the crumpled obscenities
frothing from his mouth.

"you should use
more gentle persuasion
you know!"
she yells
into the back room.

"never worked with you!"
his yell echoes
down the hall,
down decades
in doddering syllables
about 50 years.

50 years
I think,
with a darling beloved.

there is now
so much between
sounds and silences
of those words
that it has changed
the meaning,

and yet
the same words
are still said.

excuses 10

end.
my thumb
finds the button
out of habit,

the back door
out
of this conversation.

with a press,
the satellite
tether,
the last thin line
tying us,
tying me,
goes the way
of all
your other
lines,

snaps,
fizzles,
dead,
a dud firecracker.

I picture its tail
diminishing
against the black
of space,

sputtering,
stuttering,

as the syllables
of your fading
excuses.

and then I
pocket my phone,
crack a match
to life,

its head burns,
some poor
wooden semele,
illuminating the night
and fostering
all of my bad habits.

I inhale
the noxious nicotine,
deliberately
forgetting the minutes
its steals from me,
but remembering
something
even more toxic.

your lips
are still
far away
but still
speaking,
all those old accusations
attaching to me,
parasitic flukes
to my
swimming mind.

I have to keep
moving
or I will drown,

but I only
swim
in circles,
my excuses
falling out
as old fillings
into my mouth,

reminding me
of all the holes
they fill.

predators sleep 10

predators sleep,
predators sleep alone,
predators, alone, sleep in the open.

in the open,
in the open I shiver,
I shiver in the open sunlight.

open sunlight!
open sunlight windows,
sunlight windows open, collapsing stars.

collapsing stars,
collapsing stars devour,
your stare, collapsing stars, devours me.

devours me,
devours me, my pulse;
my pulse devours me in my predators sleep.

beginnings 10

naked skin,
skin naked, trembles
skin trembles, naked as ice.

as ice,
ice as earth,
ice earth as stars dim.

stars dim,
dim stars sing,
sing, dim stars, of light.

of light,
light of flowering,
flowering light of beginnings.

history repeating 10

in the pages history stretches,
I feel so little
before the indelible ink,
a fed child of their hungers.

I feel so little
of fingers that wrote
of their hungers, a fed child
that ate their futures.

their futures, that ate
a fed child of their hungers,
that wrote of fingers.
I feel so little

of their hungers, a fed child
before the indelible ink,
I feel so little
in the pages history stretches.

wild 10

wild, these private places,
the folds, creviced corners that beds
make themselves into,
archives of molted skin, of shed sanctuary,
yellow with all the suns and soil
that have trailed across their wilderness.
faint with thirst for mirages,

water will not do in this faint
wilderness, it evaporates too quickly.
lies quench better the desert, it flowers yellow;
sanctuary to light, to heat, to sighing
silences that lips need, not words that make
beds into well-walled zoos
that only have windows on the wild.

broken cup
(SPILT MILK) 10

it slips
from a suckling's
fingers,

ON ITS WAY DOWN,

spilling
milk upon
the feaux-tiled floor

THE WHITE FLYING,

spilling from her
unpracticed lips,
now rounding
the newsprint words

EACH A GLOBULAR ASTRONAUT,

sounding them out
the way they taught her
break it down
then put the pieces
together

SCATTERING IN SUDDEN

PANICKED FREEDOM,

the wars,
the murders,
the products,
the things
that cannot be
but are

FLOATING AS IF PHYSICS

HAD BUMPED ITS HEAD

AND BECOME AMNESIC,

she says them right,
and the air
and her ears agree,
but they still
garble behind her
furrowed brow

        FRANTIC AND KINETIC,

        CUP AND LIQUID HOVER

        AROUND EACH OTHER,

she blinks,
narrows her eyes
to blur these smalls
into a whole

        THEY KISS BRIEFLY

        AS GRAVITY

        REGAINS CONSCIOUSNESS,

and it seems
to come together,
between and behind
them all,
a larger shape looming,

        AND THEY ARE UNITED

        EVEN APPEARING UPRIGHT

        AND READY TO DRINK

but her mouth,
but her mind,
cannot
configure itself

        AND THEN

        SHATTERS ON IMPACT.

this deep 10

this deep,
this ache,
is an ocean
I swim under,

warm,
close,
pressing
in every inch.

a swaddling
that releases
me
from my obligation
to move

or even
consider it.

so I float.

I could break
the surface
with a curious finger
up
toward the sun,
through the skin,

and rise,

my ears
suddenly hearing
waves and wind

but here
I have the dull thumping
of my heartbeat,
of tides,
conversing,
synchronized.

up there,

my breath would begin
but as a frigid scream
of a new born
trembling,
traumatized
by its own loss of control.

if I rise,

the edge of the sea
would cut me

with the cold
and seal behind this
shivering self,

a trapped denizen
of this new world

of immediate sensations,
and raw reflexes.

not like this deep

where all is delayed,
lingering in the most loving way,

and separations
are gradual slopes
of maybes

not chasms of certainties,
where I must hurt
at every happening,

here this sea
will always be,

on me   in me   with me,

I will stay
in
this deep.

diagnosis 10

each of these
hairs,
a curled contrast,
lightning
against
the dark auburn
of older,
but fresher days.

these piercing
whites,
an electricity,
frozen memories
of the intensities
of passed
traumas,

my own
or others,

excruciatingly
drained
by my vampiric
ruminations.

all the silly
things
I worried about.
silly
because they
were merely
possible,
demented potentials
that danced digital
on the TV,

all ranting
street zealots,
pointing,
warning,
against evil,
against the end.

but not like this.

this is all
so quiet,
so politely spoken about.

doctor's appointments
made, kept
on time.
results
so patiently
awaited.

but it is
weighted

with the all
too real
eventuality
of a diagnosis.

113

invisible 10

i

bREATHELAuGH
tHINKyELLKNoW
ARGuEcARECaUSE
WAnTtAKEAsK
NeEDLOVeDREAm
eXIST

trying 10

trying hard
to not be
angry,

trying hard
to not be
bitter,

trying hard
to not be
petty,

trying hard
to not be
hard,

i can do it

but only by
trying hard

to not be.

a series of breaths 10

scent of a lilac bush
in a private corner
of the yard,
the Beatles singing
in ear-alternating
stereophonic strands
on my headphones,
their braided voices
raising my heartbeat,
weaving my possibilities,

I shut my eyes,
drink a summer sun
and breathe

in the blue sky
at a playground
10 but too old
for the jungle gym,
my hands burrowing
the infinity of a sandbox
in a child's unthinking
meditation upon
adolescent torments,
I realize
"I'll be the only
one to really care for me"
I resolve to be
more self-reliant,

I nod at my grip,
to minute granules slipping
and sigh

the window fogs
my breath is warmer
than the winter
outside the car.
my parents driving me
to the new house,
the old one too full
of happenings.
it's just easier to pack up
and take me here
among the trees
to a fairy tower
where hands can't
find my skin again,

I let them,
so tired of fingers,
and exhale

the smoke jettisons
out with my words,
as his eyes smiled
in hormonal adoration,
stoned and tongue-tied,
but my mouth is sober
with rage and rants,

and other wasted breaths
that will never have ears.
his lips wait for mine to stop.
he has another use for them.

they never did.
he found other lips,
and
I found other uses
for mine,
until they have no more
to say

or expire.

yields 10

why do my words
reproduce
so rapidly
with worry.

is that
the nature
of fertility,

fear?

fiddling fingers,
scribbling down
words
as if hammering boards
to the windows
before the storm,

or exploding
a fruiting tree
as its limbs
are cut.

why always these?

why can't
my words pronounce
the syllables
of warm cinnamon ,
of eyes admiring,
of stars blinking back,

or just
of the moments
I was
so sure of you,
so sure of me,
so sure
of us?

why is the knot
in my stomach
always tangling
on those
nots,

and the butterflies
there
scattering in a
communal panic,
blocking out
the sky
at the potential
of a predator's pounce,

and not

levitating on a leaf
among lilies?

would I have
words
without them?

storyteller 10

her eyelids
shine; mauve,
pristinely curved
slipper shells,
slipping
in and out,
in the lilt
of a doll's
long lashed,
low lidded
lullaby,

as if
in the perpetual
drowsing
in a dream
too warm
to wake from.

her voice
a lapping tide,
only briefly
alluding to itself,
to curl and carry
upon shores

what the deep
most often hides,

scattering them,
in julian curves,
on the whispering
crest of her voice,
letting the
natural course
of their rising
of their glimmer
under sun.

decide
their logic,
their grammar,
the ultimate
pattern
of their glimmer
under sun.

c0unt 10

your eyes blink
counting
the minutes,

until I realize
that you are not
really
listening.

you say
I count

too much
the events that
have happened,
are happening,

the single tragedy,
the millionth statistic,
each the same
except that our eyes
have grown tired,
and flip passed
the channel

to something
more
diverting.

even now
you are wishing
I would change
the subject,

recounting
them with
my too
numerous
ruminations

the 4 million
handcuffed
to a bedpost,

the 1 in 4
before
they're 18,

170,000
by AIDS,

a life-expectancy
of 46.

the numbers
from around
the world
crunching

under the
hard hammers
of moral
bean-counters
on their
calculators.

the true tally
counting

for nothing,

because

it doesn't happen
here,
so by all
accounts,
actual or actuarial,
it doesn't happen.

the only thing
that counts
you say
is
that I was
at least
born to a privileged
few;

that I went to school,
        20 million don't
that most
        stay home,
        work hunched over,
        or
        work
 in other positions.

not you,
you're lucky,
you should
count
your blessings,

and just be thankful
it's there
not here,
its them,
not you,

enjoy what
you have,

and that is
what
too many
are counting
upon.

koi 10

the car flew
but your eyes
swam.

just then
suddenly,
you were koi.

the sun shafts
reaching through
the sun roof
as if through
sunken coral,
shimmering

white, gold
and kept,

your eyes sunk,
your voice immersed,

on your every
movement,
on the rising, falling
crests of your hair.

a silver streak
coiling, curling
to its own
undercurrents
navigating
the dark gardens

you lilted, roared
with the radio,
every syllable
a dolphin leaping,
daring air and sea
in sonorous tides
drowning out
all storms
of open ocean.

of such seeming shallows
made a maze
by your
exploration of them.

and the sun,
the sky,

and I,

until a hook,
hooked you,
reeling into
an inlet,

merely reflections
on the rippling
surface.

the lyrics
swimming below
deep
creating their own
currents
in your consciousness,
a cloistered pond.

eventually 10

eventually
all the particles
at some instant
of time
will pass

through me.

even the newly
calculated
finite forever

is long enough
for this to happen;

that big,
that far away,
that rapidly expanding.

eventually
all possibilities
will happen
and
all nevers
will end.

eventually
my lungs
will hold
Caesar's breath,

my dustpan
will sweep up
Lennon's ashes,

and a atom
leaving my fingertip
will touch both
the place of my birth
and my death

and then move on
to more intriguing locales.

so I suppose
that
eventually

we
(or at least some part of us)
will find each other again.

sad thing 10

sad thing.
am i weak
because i want to die?
because i can't find
any reason to live?

it's not me.
it's the company i keep.

disappointed
this world,
sad thing.
empty,
full,
liars, sadists,
religious zealots
jim-jonesing
for their dose
of moral superiority.
while jabbing holes
in arms,
in hymens,
in lives;

forcing things in,
forcing things out,

sad thing,
to both incidents,
you are
incidental.

sad things
that call
themselves
men,
better thans
claiming to be
my betters

talking about
my place,
this convenient
installation
of an
all-purpose home appliance
with special attachments
for fucking.

ladies
don't kid yourself,
(sad thing-
those kids are what
they are counting upon,
more umbilicals are just
more leashes)

girls
your mama's
raising you
to be a cleaner prostitute.

sad thing,
the ones that
don't leave bruises
just
want
you

to bake them cookies
after they come home
from play.

sad thing?
you're letting them.

stalker 10

why do you pursue me
when I train my eyes
everywhere
else?

what is it about me
that draws you,
when my nods
merely, clearly
only tolerate
this terse
exchange;
a product
of upbringing,
how every little girl
is supposed to be

considerate
to every face,
an ear
to every mouth,
sympathetic
to even
her stalker.

nothing I do
makes you
go away,

I dress up,
I dress down,
you still
undress me,
I look away,
I look directly,
you still
stare,
I smile,
I grimace,
it makes
no difference,
I speak,
I'm mute,
but you'd
have to listening
to notice.

no,
nothing I do
makes you
go away.

but it isn't
about me
is it,

nothing I do
makes you

do anything.

still II 10

I sit
still,
before a red light,
a storm washes
over the roof,

your words
over me;

still,

even though
your lips
are not here
to say them.

that mouth
has amnesia
and now pretends
there is only sun
and that
it never shaped
itself
so sharply
against me.

but my memory
is not so
adaptive.

my eyes
still
occasionally leak
at inconvenient times,
usually
blinking back
the sights
you find
so blurry;

my heart
still
jumps and pounds
with frightened
little footsteps
still
trying to outrun
you.

but mostly,
still,
my throat
chokes upon
all the one-sided
conversations
caught in two-way
traffic,

I keep them
there,
stalled
and
still
no danger
to anyone
else,

and even
when I am
still
I am anything
but
still.

heavy 10

your eyes
pled to give
me sympathy,

to nod
to my weariness
as fully justified,
to sigh
to my pain
as if you felt it,

the open wound
too many times
bandaged
then torn back
before it could heal,

the wrappings
the loose slip-shod
trappings
I tied clumsily
around it;

each artificial gesture
and insincere word
expected
and
acquiesced to,

bacterial particles
digging them selves
into my gut
like grit
without a pearl
but
instead infection,
writing itself
in scars upon
each
sense
and memory,

creating tissue
both too numb
and all too feeling.

so now
sun only burns,
touch only tears,
and even
the vaporous
weight
of your waiting
gaze

is too heavy.

black hole afternoon 10

the sky is pressing
down
on every inch
of my skin,

as if a star
has died,
taking all its light
in the collapse
under its
own weight,

leaving

only its
gravity and heat.

beneath
the orchids wilt
into a cowering curl,
their petals
having evolved
in a place
requiring less
strength,

even the air
is too
much for their
frailty.

my neurons
languish with them.
the space
between
each connection
that has always
allowed
a Brownian buffer
of latent thought

has now
solidified,
a mass of
compressed
molecules.

the panic
of maybes
is no more.

the sky is not falling,

it has already
shattered
leaving now
the tedium
of maneuvering
around the shards

with a barefoot
being.

the words
on all the signs
are melting
away,

the painted edges
still sharp
but
bleeding
together
in my eyes.

even the sun
that pokes
through the
drowsy storm,
that is only lazily
considering rain,
adds an
obscene brightness
to the most ordinary.

yellow umbrellas
whose hue
mocks the mortality
of fading flowers,

shimmering cars
that gleam
like water
but will never
quench,
for all the places
that normally
remember showers
are suffering
from a crackled
amnesia.

and there
is the smell
of garbage,
unfinished food;
too much
for even
the habitually
fattened families
who passing by me,
somehow,
do not feel
the same gravity,

who laugh
in lighted syllables
even as
the singularity
grows.

127

swallow 10

my words are lost
flitting in
a silence
that has, at least,
the comfort
of not hearing
the finality
of what they
have to say.

and yours
molest my ears,
pursuing me
in this only
private grotto
and force
all I think
upon the air,
smoking all
my swallows
from their cave
in an exodus
for your tourist
entertainment.

for you cannot
no, will not,
look upon the hole
you have carved
into me
using time,
rain
and my own
geological weakness
to cut it deep.

its darkness
is yours,
the mirror
of your own empty,
except that mine
still has
fluttering life
within it
giving even my
still lips
more eloquence
than your mere
echo,

the repetition
of old excuses.

and both our
voices know
of your crimes,
by omission
by commission.

you want
my words to fly
so you can
net them,
cut their wings,
cage them,

and teach them
your echoes.

but I will
not speak.
instead

I
swallow.

howl 10

a wolf's
low murmuring
in the moonlight.

the guttural
slips from
my throat
and crystallizes
with my breath
upon the air,

then melts
in Luna's
glowing gaze.

she never
glares
too sharply
upon me

but with soft lids
her eyes shimmer
inducing
ice to simmer
on limbs,
on leaves,
seducing
all Cimmerians
who found
more light
in this night

than in day.

her clarity
carries
their voices
with mine,
mournful
but not
for morning,

but for
an answer
that is not
just an echo,
but still
the same

in its
distant moaning
that will
close the miles,
open the darkness,

at this edge
of the round
world,
a horizon
that even sun
will not sink to.

we live
untimid mortals
alone
but no lonelier
than sound
can carry,

each reciprocal
sonorous vocal
our common ground.

raising my head
breathing sky
with my skin,
and time
with a heartbeat,

I howl

to all the
other parts of me.

129

forgive and forget 10

where did this
moment really start?

when I screamed
as air first
scorched
my liquid lungs?

when that
sound later
articulated into
words

that soon learned
they had no ears?

and when
they found ears
their syllables
became
so twisted
by the silences
they had maneuvered
around
that they longer
pronounced
the same meaning?

all those
shhhhh!'s
as if the whole
world was a library.

not that the sound
of them mattered,
the answer
was the same:

forgive and forget.

I take the
suggestion
and try
to achieve
the bliss of
the amnesic
in ritual distraction,
well-formed forgetting,

but each
present moment
suggests
a before

and a before-that.

all those appointments
I have to keep,
all those names
that want to remember me

when I'm trying
so hard
to forget.

and each step
must have
a future
or I will fall

face first
into the pavement.

am I to wonder
how my nose
suddenly became
so bloody

but not wonder
any further than
that

for fear of all
the futures
that bleeding suggests?

(being sure not
to cry out of course
for that would be
disruptive
but instead
to quietly calculate
how I am to build
a life of daisy-chained
empties)

then
get up
brush myself
off
with the brush
off

forgive and forget.
forgive and forget.

as if repeating
them
was a sorcery
to close
an artery.

no.
it does not work
no matter how
many times
I say it.

they are just
fugue filled
syllables
keeping me
from saying
anything
else.

shhhh!!

terror Fermi 10

the bounded
nutshell
is breaking

and the infinite space
is pouring
in
with the possibility
of nevers.

"Where is everybody?"

the words echo against
the thin skin
over a black sea
stagnant with
ancient flickers

is it the age that makes
it silent?
is the depth too much to
fathom
or is it that each light
lasts
only as long as an intellect
fans it?

and is ours dimming?

oh so many ways to go…

a Methuselah complex
becomes
a Malthusian mouse trap,
because so many
are pro-life
but not
pro-life-cycle,

until hollow Earth
collapses
under the weight
of our brutish brood

that assumed
uranium
favored ideologies
and
pathogens
had sympathies

or that raptures
would come
on the tails of comets
and let them escape
all those consequences.

evolved too well,
evolved too little,
the Machiavellian
become the majority
via unnatural selection,

each a prince
in his own mind
and entitled
to all the privileges.

the whimper
and not the bang?

will all those
cities and satellites
just power down
because the caretakers
had become careless,

devolvedand doddering
with all our dependencies?

is that why
the infinite
is silent?

or are they
all just whispering
behind our backs?

don't look up 10

the empiricals and
the evangelicals
are talking about the end.

all the ways
the sky will fall.
the earth will rise,

the burnings,
the freezings,

I swear they're smiling!
their gazes gleam
at the countdowns
of shortening days,

relieved of all those
far tomorrows,
the retirements,
the 401k's
that require proper planning.

don't look up.

the sun
will sear your eyes
the moon
with its round and fragile,
will remind you
of a blue droplet
spinning,

and you,
caught in its
centrifugal
but so far
from any center,
of ever being central.

don't look up.

for your god
cut from the clouds,
a paper doll

dressed
in local fashion,
addressed
too readily in emergency
but,as all those
bureaucratic hierarchies,
those legions of lazy
guardian angels,

slow to respond.

the Haitians and the Creoles
are still waiting for their
prayers to be processed
in triplicate by the trinity
and returned.

not yet.
check the mail tomorrow.

or maybe
the constellations
are still contemplating
our positions,

I guess it's all just one more
argument against
faster-than-light travel,
which means the aliens
aren't coming either
so

don't look up.

only the blue,
only the stars,
only the rain,
only the cumulus accumulating,

carrying on the echo
of the big bang,

all the real reasons
to look up.

splinter 10

there's a cut in my heel
that I keep
stepping on,
some splinter
sneakily slipped
in

one
day while I,
remembering
grass and sun,
foolishly went
barefoot.

it settled
snug
into its new home
of cutis and callous,

all those layers
of me,
compiled
after all those miles

unfelt,
forgotten,

but now each step
pierces

as the sliver
tosses and turns
in its hibernation.

its restless
limbs
poking into me
as it
kicks out nightmares.

and when
I dig in after
it

it burrows deeper,
carving out
new labyrinths
into my geology

far into
that pink flesh
inhabited by nerves
that only remember
young steps
and never numbed
but only succumbed
to a slow burial,

and now they are awake,

each one
a screaming infant
upon rebirth
and
my foot
is red and raw
collaged
in dingy band-aids

that keep falling off.

I feel it.
the splinter

turning again,

maybe
this time
a nightmare about tweezers.

I will let it sleep.

I guess
we'll both
just have

to get used to it.

fruition 11

so long in
culminating,
cultivating,

my thoughts
are a ripe green
avocado

fatty,
smooth;

ice cream
before
ice
ceased to be
a commodity,
an oddity,

an artifact
of our artificial jungles.

i must scoop
out the heart
and eat directly
from the skin

to taste
these ponderings
wondering
upon my tongue

i press them against
the roof of my mouth
squeezing out
all the tears
i can get from
the flesh
of this
alligator pear.

such textures
are rare in nature

when all
is substance,
is subsistence;

an existence
never full,
never filling.

this pome is a poem

that once fed
lethargic, giant
ground sloths
now extinct,

and became
forbidden fruit
to the Aztecs kings,
also extinct,

now feeding me,
(who will someday
follow
edentates and empires)

but for now
it is a meal of words,
sensations;
mostly unpronounceable,

and even with the
brown round seed
in my hand

and all of my modern
conveniences,

it will take
years, warmth
and patience

to grow more.

back among the monsters 10

when I was
young,

I used to dream

of zombies.

not
the camp,
the dull-eyed
dim-witted
mounds
of flesh.

you know,
those
not so well crafted
B-movie-drafted
drones
with moans
and a leisurely pace.

we would laugh
at them.

fake blood,
spurting slapstick
of clumsy carcasses

falling over each other
for the buxom blond
with high heels
and a bad ankle,

her only appeal
was a good meal.

it was all
so amusing,
so unreal.

and we could
always
turn the TV
off.

no.
the ones
that trudged
no so cinematically
projected
upon my eyelids

were different,

or maybe i
was different.

the plot
was the same:

cornered, surrounded.
ominous thuds.
lingering laments
        behind every wall.
dead fingers prying
        at the locked door,
        in lethargic,
        relentless pursuit.
(after all,
why should they rush?
        they always had me

outnumbered.)

and their faces
came from the local graveyard
of my waking life
    parents,
    friends,
    enemies

in the end
all wanting
the same thing from me.

and I had to wait

curled in a closet,
contemplating
every tooth and tear,
my pulse pounding
    in my ear.

then the boards
    would splinter
    the hinges
        would give

    and supine steps
        would soon find
        the soup on.
sometimes
I'd find myself
among them,
shoulder to shoulder,
making my breath shallow,
    my eyes milky,
    my face empty,

so I could pass,

because
all it would take
was a simple scrape
to make it real.

then again,
maybe that would've
been easier
then finding
new places to hide.

they don't chase me
anymore.

I commute to them.

precious 11

it glimmers
and a worn hand
pulls it from
its igneous sky,

a star
that has fallen up,

the planet's heart
bleeding
molten
then frozen
into earthen night.

the calloused hand
caresses its cold

all the years
it has taken,
the few days
it will buy.

his flesh
almost as dim
as the void
around him

curling around
this precious.

the only
light
in all this darkness

and yet
it had brought
this pitch
that clung
to him,
to the air,
to everything
but its slick surface.

adama,
diamond.

the perfect beauty
that refracted
outward
the imperfections
of his species,
the wonders and horrors.

these glistening jewels
had many hues.
some yellow,
blue, green,
champagne
and white,

but this one
was blood,
no matter
its color.

he had seen it
glisten,
trickling
from his own hands.

in these places
color matters.

so much,
too much

long ago,
a black boy
at an orange river
found the
star of Africa
and the dark continent
flooded white
with hands
then
red,

reaching
for this
precious;

for the rarity
that fed
egos and ideologies

and Earth's axis turned
pulled by avarice
away from Polaris
to this place,
to a new north.

now
every one
could wear constellations
they would settle upon
slender ivory necks,
adorn dainty fingers,
and
cut into futures
unthought-of.

he runs
clenching
it close,
its cut
slicing his palm,

but he dares not

relax his grip
for what would slip
through it.

it has traveled
near-forevers,

his life
a half-flickered pulse
to its breath,

but it would buy
eternities
for him,
for his family,
the tiny eons
of happiness

that too only came
precious
few
from much digging.

in the black of his hand
it sparkled,
the sum
of internal reflection
that the cutter will study
to pull from it,
a gem.

but each strength
has its own weakness

a miscalculated cleave
and it
shatters,

this precious,
gone

billions of years,
250 tons,
just for
one.

the miner holds his breath
at the thought
of all that would shatter
with it,

and then
runs
faster.

that day 08

Behind every word she read, the few hypocrisies she refused to commit - that day. It would also be the cause of her destruction. It hardened and expanded in her throat forcing inexplicable tears out of her eyes. And why she couldn't believe any promise.

She remembered a summer; a pink and purple twilight. It hung in the windows as the other children watched t.v. and glasses clinked to intellectual debates over the kitchen table. There were many families in the house now, a gathering of lower-middle class college graduates and their well fed, well read children. The house held the thick happiness of a dozing cat. slow. content. tangible upon the skin.

The kids watched cartoons, but she was precocious, always curious as to what adults talked about when children weren't there. Drinking loosened their jaws and dulled their attention. She slipped into the kitchen unnoticed and flattened herself to the wall and became wall paper.

Those expecting crudities at this point will not hear them. These were tea totelers and wine made their words LONGER not shorter. It stretched each syllable to its breaking point and even invented new words. She listened to their every surface.

It was an election year. They were talking about an actor who had become governor and now wanted to be president. They questioned his qualifications and experience.
"You want his finger hovering over the button?!!"

The button. She knew that phrase. She always pictured some big red button like a fire alarm. It meant a nuclear bomb. The concept was not unfamiliar to her, even at age six. A large explosive, a big boom.

The conversation then spoke about a foreign place with an even odder name. She had never heard it before. Hiroshima; where "the bomb" had been dropped. Until that moment, she had never known that the bomb had ever been used. It was always an abstract threat.

But then, she heard them describe: A normal sunny day, that became brighter. A flash.

People became shadows. Eyes melted in their sockets.Some mere burned only to learn that survival meant they would die slower. and their children would know it to. and their children. and irreparably scorched earth.

She had never known that. Now a divided world had more than one bomb. It had hundreds of maybe-days like that. in silos. on submarines. enough to destroy earth.. "one hundred and seventy-four times over..."

She thought once was enough.

But a dissenting voice chimed in: How we had to. Because of Pearl Harbor. Because of Nazis. She knew that word too. She knew their uniforms, their "goose-stepping" across t.v. and theater screens as villains. The bad guys, no more ominous to her than a cowboy with a black hat. But there was more.

The word "Holocaust". The word "millions". She couldn't even comprehend such large numbers, and each one was a person. murdered. by killers. by people who watched the killers and did nothing. She understood that. She'd seen kids torture animals in the neighborhood, mostly frogs or snakes. A few kids laughed, some giggled. But the rest were silent with sad eyes,including her, wanting to speak and some not saying anything.

She'd seen it in others eyes when it was her turn to be picked on. The meek "Stop it guys..." that faded off into shrugged shoulders.

It had never occurred to her, that adults acted like that too.
They had their own version of bullies.
Millions.

And then someone said it. "...at least Hitler never got the bomb...".
The words didn't register at first.
She slipped out the front door, absorbing them.

The sky was still pink and the air indistinguishable from her skin. No mosquitoes and the fireflies were just beginning a lightshow in the nearby field where kids played kick-the-can.
A perfect summer night.

"never got the bomb"

not yet
She realized. She knew there would always be more Hitlers and more wide-eyed, shut-mouthed bystanders. She played with them. They picked on her. She was growing up with them.
And the bomb had turned into hundreds, then thousands. More than enough for just one wrong person.

She looked at the sky and tried to imagine it black, at the trees and see ash. At the passing people on the sidewalk and see shadows. All that was green would be gone and all that was flesh, fragility. But there was worse. For all the worlds pettiness, even she knew there were rare kindnesses. When someone would stop the bullying.

Adults had those too. She'd heard the names. Gandhi, Martin Luther King, JFK. Their names were not uttered in reverence or awe, but with a personal affection. As if they had sat down at that table one night too. And the way people shook their heads, still, at their deaths, like whispering about some secret shameful act. How they were killed by those who, for some inexplicable reason, wanted hate. The world Hitler wanted. She guessed that kindness must have made people like that remember something painful, so they never wanted to feel or even see it.

But there was also the kindnesses that didn't make it into books or on t.v. The ones people did every day just by being patient. Going to a job they hated to buy food and a home for their family. Buying presents they couldn't afford because, well, just because.

But these would no longer exist in a world with no memory. Paper burns, shadows have no mouths. All that sacrifice would just become one more inch of ash.
For nothing.
She wanted to cry, but couldn't. Her eyes ached with it. But instead there was a shiver, as if a layer of skin had just been burnt off and left her cold and naked.

please no...
don't let it...
she prayed in a place she felt no god...
I'll do anything...
I'll die if you want me to , just don't ...

But she couldn't really believe that anyone
was listening.
But there was time, she hoped, to learn;
to figure it out,
to understand why and walk away
from that day.

truth 11
(poem for an object)

I see it.
you see it.
they see it.
but
somewhere
in
between,

it
still has a secret.

life story 08

and then there was	light
and then there was	love
and then there was	hate
and then there was	will
and then there was	won't
and then there was	love
and then there was	silence

www.ingramcontent.com/pod-product-compliance
Lightning Source LLC
Chambersburg PA
CBHW052104090426
42741CB00009B/1675